A Strange Unmaking

A Strange Unmaking
Ten Years in Colombia

Fiona Lyn Christie

ISBN-13: 9798666039717

Blogs were originally published on
www.fcinmc.blogspot.com
and
www.astrangeunmaking.co.uk.

Bible quotes are taken from THE HOLY BIBLE, NEW INTERNATIONAL VERSION®, NIV® Copyright © 1973, 1978, 1984, 2011 by Biblica, Inc.™ Used by permission. All rights reserved worldwide.

The C.S. Lewis quote is taken from *Mere Christianity* (London: William Collins, 2016, pg. 205).

Acknowledgements

Thank you to SelfPubBookCovers.com/RLSather for the beautiful cover.

I can't begin to name everybody who helped me to serve in Colombia but I will mention my dear colleagues in Vive and the Latin Link community, both in Colombia and internationally, my sending church, St Thomas' in Edinburgh, and my church in Medellín, *La Primera Iglesia Presbiteriana*, my faithful and generous supporters, and my family and friends.

But I will single out my parents for their unfailing and uncomplaining support. This book is lovingly dedicated to them.

TABLE OF CONTENTS

Introduction

"YOU MUST DO something you're afraid of," said the pastor from Cairo, addressing a meeting I attended in Edinburgh in early 2006. He added, "That is how faith grows." I knew I was afraid of travelling to Colombia. I had dear friends there who had often invited me to visit them, and they assured me that the country wasn't nearly as dangerous as the media portrayal of it at the time. But in the early years of the 21st century, Colombia was still notorious for violence, drug trafficking and what scared me the most, kidnapping. The film *The Motorcycle Diaries*, the story of Che Guevara's travels through South America as a young man, had stirred in me the desire to return to the continent I had left as a child. Now I couldn't use my fear as an excuse not to go. A few days later I bought my plane tickets and in the summer of 2006, I headed off for a three-week holiday, little guessing what lay ahead.

I was already entranced by the green of the countryside and the courtesy of the people by the second day of my holiday when my host, the rector of the Bible Seminary of Colombia in Medellín at the time, asked me if I would consider setting up English courses in the Seminary. I said something pious like, "I'd have to pray about that," but a few days later, looking out over the garden of my friends' house, I heard a voice in my head say, "You know you're going to do this."

In early 2008 I returned to Colombia to begin a ten-year adventure in the most vibrant and challenging place I had ever encountered. I soon realized that Colombia was going to stretch my faith in ways I hadn't imagined, and that I was undergoing "a strange unmaking", a breaking and re-making that would be painful but ultimately fruitful. Colombia also gave me stories, insights and observations for a blog I wrote most days and for my quarterly newsletter. Poems, Biblical reflections and observations gushed out of me into my journals and notebooks and onto little scraps of paper that I am still finding tucked into books years later.

This book is a collection of my writings during the ten years I was in Colombia. I have grouped my blog posts by topic and interspersed them with poems and other previously unpublished reflections, occasionally providing some context in italics.

My life in Colombia was a roller coaster ride: at times I was riding high, often I was in the depths of despair, but God was always with me, and it is to Him that all the glory belongs.

The Beginning

Poem for a New Life

THE MONTHS BEFORE *I left Scotland in 2008 were full of mundane tasks to be checked off multiple to-do lists. I felt my arrival in Colombia should herald a new, creative phase in my life.*

> I used to write poetry
> But then it dried up.
> And my life became
> a list of things to do.
> Let it be a sonnet again.
> Or at the very least
> A Haiku.

Gabriel García Márquez, Colombia's Nobel Laureate in Literature, is reported to have said, "All I ever wrote was journalism." You may know that he was a leading exponent of a style of writing called magical realism, in which supernatural events are reported alongside the mundane. He was making a point about the Colombian reality, and it's true, the most extraordinary things happen in Colombia every day, the wonderful and the horrific, jostling together in the most disconcerting way.

I did not write any sonnets or Haikus in Colombia, but I was never short of a blog entry.

Digging

I WROTE DIGGING *in the early days of my time in Colombia and the idea is borrowed from writings of C.S. Lewis. In Lewis' metaphor, as we embark on our Christian lives, we find that God tidies us up in ways that seem sensible. Only later does He begin to make painful changes that we find difficult to understand. Lewis, himself borrowing from George MacDonald, writes in Mere Christianity, "You thought you were being made into a decent little cottage: but He is building a palace. He intends to come and live in it Himself."*

In 2008, I had no idea what I was getting into. But it seems I had an inkling that it was going to be painful:

The spade is digging in to the packed ground.
The eternal gardener turns over the dark earth of my heart.

He has good seed in His hand.

I would have been happy with a window box,
but he wants to plant an estate.

A Strange Unmaking

After six months in Colombia, I wrote in my journal:

For me, Colombia has been a strange unmaking.

I believed my own publicity and did not expect to suffer like this, unaware that I had spent two years digging a hole, into which I promptly fell.

For two or three months, I felt as if I was on the edge of the ocean, struggling to get to my feet when – wham – the next wave came along.

And then came the retreat and I got some space to rest and think, and God lifted me out of the pit.

And I lived more peacefully.

But I am still picking up and carrying the little stones that are the suffering, second hand, of this nation.

To be re-made, I had to be un-made. And God sent me to Colombia to be re-made. But not before the ocean waves had smashed me to pieces.

First Impressions

I STARTED MY BLOG a few months after I arrived in Colombia in January 2008 and often used it to try to make sense of the strange new world I had landed in.

RULES AND REGULATIONS

I have had two similar experiences recently that made me reflect on the place of rules here, on being foreign, and on the importance of relationships.

One was in a bank. I needed to pay some cash into an account, but was told that this service was only available to people who have accounts with the bank, which I don't. I asked the teller what I should do, and she said, "*Tranquila, te colaboro.*" (= Don't worry, I'll help you.) She helped me with the form, took my cash, and said that next time I would have to find a bigger branch, where I would be allowed to carry out the transaction.

Another time, I needed to return some clothes to a supermarket. I cheerfully presented the items and the receipt at the appropriate desk. The two women got very agitated that the clothes WEREN'T IN A BAG. Apparently, you have to bring unwanted goods in a carrier bag that you have to get sealed by the security guard on your way in. What to do? I had a brainwave. I would go and buy something, get a plastic bag, put my unwanted items in it, go out of the shop and get the security guard to seal it. When I said this to the women, they laughed and said, "*Tranquila.*" Next time, I would have to do things the proper way, but this time, as I was clearly foreign and didn't know the rules, they would exchange my goods for me. Here, it seems, personal connection is everything and rules don't matter very much. This is very nice for me - all I have to do when I confront bureaucracy is look stricken and speak stumbling Spanish - but I don't know if it is good for a nation, in the long run.

FOOD

One thing I have noticed here is a subtly different attitude to food. This is because, in a land of plenty, where the supermarkets are as well stocked as any in Europe, people around me are going hungry. One consequence is that food is never wasted: a colleague of mine froze the leftovers from an event she was at in the United States, knowing they would be thrown out, and brought them back in her hand luggage to share with friends here.

Some students in the Seminary pay for a breakfast and lunch six days a week, but often can't afford anything to eat in the evening, and some families are subsisting on bread and milk. But, Colombians are generally so positive and upbeat, that I am only realising very slowly how much need there is right on my doorstep. Sharing with those in need takes on a different dimension when it is people you see every day and not the faceless poor at the other end of a charity donation.

DEMOCRATIC SECURITY

I've been told that President Uribe's policy of democratic security has made the cities here safer and the countryside more dangerous. The result is that you can live most of the time in Medellín without the reality of Colombia's conflict impinging on you at all, if you ignore the ragged, displaced people at the traffic lights begging for help with their misspelled signs. But every so often something happens to make you aware that this is a country still suffering an extremely damaging civil conflict.

Here are three examples:

On television, between adverts for shampoo and breakfast cereals, there are adverts calling members of the armed groups to demobilize, with the slogan *Demobilization is the way out*.

Rummaging among the toys in a shop on the Coast, I found a little model plastic soldier with what I took to be a mine detector in his hand, part of the landscape in a country with the third greatest number of land mines in the world.

And finally, the anti-explosive dog I spotted playing his part in keeping the crowds safe during Medellín's spectacular flower festival in August.

And how do Colombians cope with the war as an ever-present backdrop to their lives? By laughing! They are the most cheerful people I have ever met and they can laugh at anything. Is this evidence of the triumph of the human spirit in the face of adversity or a dysfunctional response, storing up psychological problems for generations to come? I can't quite decide.

IF I HEAR ANOTHER STORY ABOUT A DISMEMBERED BODY, I'LL SCREAM

Forming close friendships in Colombia is harder than you might think, given that Colombians are such a friendly people. When people start to share their lives with me, instead of helping us find shared interests or points of contact, their stories of utter horror and anguish often leave me reeling.

HELP ME!

I am on a bus. A well-dressed man flags it down and says to the driver, *"Colabórame."* I learned this extremely useful word on my third day here, and it means, "Help me, if necessary by bending the rules." In this case the man means, "Let me ride for free." The driver agrees and the man makes the trip to the bottom of the hill standing in the open doorway of the bus. When we reach the supermarket at the bottom of the hill, the bus stops to let the man off. But the man wants to extend his free ride a little. It seems he wants to be dropped off at the end of the bus stop, not the beginning, so he doesn't have to walk so far to the next bus. The bus driver waves him off angrily, and then looks round at us passengers, as if to say, 'what a cheek'. This cheek is a very Colombian trait and is called being *conchudo*. I don't think it has rubbed off on me yet.

CLASH OF THE WORLDVIEWS

Once a week I help on a project to take bread and hot chocolate to some poor people who live in the centre of Medellín. Because it is startlingly different from the normal tourist experience, a lot of foreigners get taken to visit the project, something I dubbed poverty tourism, thinking I was coining a phrase. In fact, this concept already exists. I was taken along to visit this project when I was here on holiday in 2006 and it made such an impact on me that I came back. So although I have some doubts about the whole idea of poverty tourism, I keep taking people along. We start in a run-down hotel, and then spend a couple of hours on the streets, among the drug addicts, prostitutes, glue-sniffing street kids, and people who make their living recycling rubbish.

A few weeks ago, a Dutch guy came along. He got chatting to one of the street people and when his Spanish ran out, I was called in to translate. The conversation went something like this:

Street Guy: Ask him if he is a Christian.
Dutch Guy: No, I'm not, but I have a lot of respect for Christian values.
Street Guy: Ask him if he wants to get to know Jesus.
Dutch Guy: Not right now. I am not saying that Christianity is not a true religion but it is not for me right now.

European post-modernism meets Colombian faith; the result: mutual incomprehension.

THE VOCABULARY OF THE CONFLICT

The many decades of conflict in Colombia have produced a whole set of vocabulary to describe the many strange and terrifying things that go on here.

Protection money is called *la vacuna* (the vaccination). The people collecting it might be *la guerrilla,* or *los paramilitares* (the paramilitaries), who have now morphed into the *paracos,* a contraction of *paramilitares* and *narcotraficantes* (the drug traffickers). When they are captured they might become *canjeable* (swappable), which means they could be exchanged for the many hostages held by the FARC, unless they decide to take up the offer of a place back in society by renouncing violence and coming clean about their crimes, in which case they become *reinsertados* (the reinserted). Their victims are the *desplazados* (the displaced), or street people, drug dealers and prostitutes who die in the chillingly euphemistic *limpieza social* (social cleansing). If crimes are committed by people who are 'just' criminals without any political motivation, that's called *delincuencia común* (ordinary delinquency), and if the conflict impinges on your daily life, you talk about being affected by *orden público* (public order), a phrase which means exactly the opposite. To talk about a particularly difficult time in Colombian history (the 1950s), people say *La Violencia,* which is neither euphemistic nor ironic.

First I misunderstood what this language meant, and then I deciphered it. Then I used it in a straightforward way and now I've started to use it to make jokes, so it's probably time to go home.

NOT NICE!

I recently happened to meet someone from northern Europe, let's say, who has been in Colombia for a month. We were just making small talk and I asked her what she thought about Colombia, and she said, "It's nice." Granted she wasn't speaking her native language but even so, the word *nice* has been jangling in my head ever since. Nice? Colombia is many things – beautiful, heart-breaking, green, rich, varied, violent, vibrant, tragic, dazzling, infuriating, beguiling, maddening, fertile, welcoming, cruel, blessed, cursed, gorgeous, scarred... but nice? No, not nice.

The First Time I went to the Coast

DURING MY FIRST TWO YEARS *in Colombia I spent most of my time developing English courses for the students of the Bible Seminary of Colombia. But in June 2008, I went on a month-long mission trip to displaced communities in different parts of the Atlantic Coast. This experience made a huge impression on me and in some ways marked the direction of the next few years of my life. But I was terribly anxious about the trip before we left:*

JOURNAL – 7/06/08

A week before the mission and I wake up every morning with a sore stomach and weight on my head. I was pleased with my insight that I needed – all I needed – was to live close to Jesus – and then found I wasn't doing it.

JOURNAL – 13/6/08

In many ways you could hardly call me a scatterbrain but scattered is exactly what my brain is. It's as if there is a little stenographer making a running commentary of my thoughts. In the 45 minutes since I got up I have had 50 different thoughts already in my head.

In preparation for our trip, I obediently packed exactly what was on the kit list, foolishly trusting that I could get by in the searing heat of the Coast with just five T-shirts! That would have worked if I could have washed them every few days but that wasn't so easy.

My notebook from the mission is full of very practical notes: an itinerary of all the days, some notes from the training, an outline of the security situation at the time, the names of the armed groups operating in the area, hour by hour plans from the week I was in charge of a team, and shopping lists.

Most poignant were the lists of the people I met:

Ana Lin: displaced in 2000, 7 children, no help.
Milena: a speech/language impairment.
Elivara: son in prison.
Luris: murdered son.
Girl in pink: pregnant.
Enith: recently displaced, miscarried.

On my return to Medellín, I tried to communicate something of the experience in several blogs:

TRIP TO THE COAST

I have been away in Córdoba, the region north of Medellín, for a month. I made a last-minute decision not to take my camera, a decision I didn't regret, as I was able to engage with everything I saw directly, without wondering if it would make a good photo. I experienced enough 'bloggable' material to last me a year, so watch this space. For now, it's enough to say that I am safely home in Medellín, brown, exhausted and thankful. As we drove into Medellín, I thought, oh, this feels like home, until I was accused of looking like an Anglo-Saxon by a taxi-driver, who subsequently ripped me off!

IN PRAISE OF DENIM

While I am working out what to say about the experience of being with some of Colombia's displaced communities, permit me a word or two in praise of denim. The final week of our month in Córdoba, I wore my jeans for seven days in a row, four of them on a construction site. In that time I helped to dig a 1.5-metre-deep hole, sieved sand to make cement, mixed cement and laid bricks, some of the time on rickety scaffolding. To get to where we were working (building toilets in a displaced community called Santa Rosa) we had to travel about 20 minutes by motorbike, a journey that included having to splash our way through two huge puddles. And my jeans didn't get dirty! They just changed colour. So hail, denim, king of hardwearing, dirt-resistant fabrics. I salute you!

DISPLACEMENT

It's impossible to engage with the current Colombian reality without confronting the issue of internal displacement. Up to four million people have been violently forced from their homes over the last 20 years. I had read a little about the issue before going to Córdoba and tried to make sense of it in terms of the Scottish Highland Clearances and the migrations to the big cities that I have seen in South Africa. But of course, nothing prepares you for the reality: a community of thousands of people living in roughly-made huts, many with only plastic sheeting for walls; children running to the roadside with bowls in their hands, begging for food; a mother cooking a meal of a few eggs for her three children by the light of a single candle. What made the biggest impression on me was spending time with displaced people, listening to their stories, trying to grasp their profound sense of loss and the intense struggle to survive they face every day. Now I can't think about displacement in terms of statistics, or of a perplexing social phenomenon. When I think about displacement, I see faces, faces of people whose names I know: Orora, Yefer Andrés, César, Camila Andrea, Enith, Ricardo, Tito, Aron, Jorge, Jenys, Luis Felipe, John, Ruth. It has become much more personal and much more troubling.

Several months later I got the opportunity to visit the Coast again:

RETURN TO THE COAST

Last weekend I got the opportunity to return to Córdoba, where I spent a month this summer. It was great to go back to the community of Santa Rosa, where the toilet block we worked on is now nearly finished. The people there seem quite positive; their crops are growing and they have just about enough land to support themselves.

It was a different story in another, longer-established community of displaced people I visited for the first time. They

21

live in well-built concrete houses but have little land and no work. They are hungry. So imagine our reaction when the pastor of the little church asked if we could help them buy a sound system for the church.

How would you have responded?

a) How absurd! Your people need food, clothes and work. Surely a sound system is an expensive luxury and should be way down your list of priorities.

b) Mmmmm. Interesting. Why is a sound system of such importance to you, given the other needs you face?

c) Of course. If that is what you perceive as a need, who are we to question that? Let's see what we can do to find you the resources for a sound system.

d) Why can't you see us as people, and not just as potential sources of money?

I still haven't worked out what the right answer is.

This post prompted some responses and I felt I needed to say a bit more about the situation the community faced:

FOLLOW-UP

Thank you to those who commented on the last post. I feel I want to say a little something in defence of the pastor in the displaced community we visited who asked if we could help him buy a sound system for his church. The community's great need is for land, about five hectares for every family, so that they can be self-sufficient in food. There are 60 families in that community and land costs about £2,500 a hectare at today's exchange rate. Even with my shaky arithmetic, I can work out

22

that that comes to a whopping three-quarters of a million pounds. Until someone comes along with that kind of cash, maybe a sound system is a modest and realistic request, which is not to say that it needs to be a priority for me.

A year later, I reported:

SOUND SYSTEM UPDATE

If you have been reading this blog since last year, you may remember the discussion about whether the pastor of a church in a displaced community was right to ask for a sound system. Well, someone reading the blog decided they wanted to help, which was my cunning plan all along, and on 12th June, the community of Nueva Esperanza (New Hope) got their sound system. They are thrilled. If you would like to buy them land, get in touch!

I was able to channel giving so that some displaced communities had sound systems but no one ever got in touch to offer to buy land!

The Glass Potter

In April 2008, I went on a retreat with staff and students from the Seminary where I wrote this little story as a reflection on 2 Corinthians 4:7: "But we have this treasure in jars of clay to show that this all-surpassing power is from God and not from us." It doesn't really make much sense but I like the basic idea.

I came to the village in the evening. I asked the first person I saw, an old man sitting on a rough wooden bench, if he knew where the glass potter lived. He pointed to a small cottage at the end of the main street. I knocked cautiously at the door. A voice bade me enter. I pushed the door open, and stood astounded in the doorway. On shelves, on the table, on the floor, in every corner of the room, glass jars stood, and in each, a candle shone. The effect was mesmerising. I noticed a door at the back of the room. I walked through the gallery of light to the room at the back – a workshop with all the tools of the potter's trade – a wheel, wire to cut through the clay, the damp clay itself in sacks.

The potter was at work, forming a pot on his wheel. The clay was of reddish earth.

So stunned was I by the room of light that I forgot my carefully prepared words of greeting and could only blurt out, "Are you the potter who turns earth into glass?"

He smiled and nodded.

"But how can that be?" I asked.

"It's simple really. Every day, I work on the pots, shaving a little bit off here and there. They get thinner and thinner as the years go on until one day they are ready to become glass."

"But how does that happen?"

"Oh, I just move them to the front room and there they can fully show the glory of the light inside them."

"Just by moving them to the front room?"

"Yes, that is all it takes. Of course the trick is knowing the exact moment the pot is ready."

I marvelled at these words but saw that I would not get further by questioning the patient potter. I watched him at work for a few moments then walked back through to the room of glory. I noticed that some jars were bigger than others, that some were in strange forms, and that in some you could see cracks that had been carefully patched. The most badly damaged were the ones that shone most beautifully because their flaws meant the light was refracted in many and various ways.

I am dust

I AM DUST.
A skilful potter
gathered up this clay,
and formed this jar.
Put a spark of light within,
began to grind the jar
and fan the flame.

My life

I WROTE THIS PRAYER on a little holiday I had after the mission trip to the Coast.

A thousand pieces of coloured glass, waiting for the Craftsman to finish the mosaic. The back of the tapestry, trusting that the front makes a picture. The words of the fridge magnets, hoping that the Poet can make them rhyme.

You, Lord Jesus, creator and sustainer of life.
You, Spirit of Life, bearer of truth, comforting presence.
You, Father of All, steadfast in love, author of all mercy.

Take the pieces of my life and make something new. Untangle the threads and make them into something beautiful.

Encounters with Children

CHILDREN EVERYWHERE CAN BE CUTE and say funny things, but somehow Colombian children were particularly enchanting. Here are some of my encounters with children:

ENCOUNTER

I met a little girl, well, not so little, she's nine. I introduced myself as Fiona, "You know, Fiona, like Princess Fiona in Shrek." For some reason, she smiled, and stretched out her hand to stroke my head. It was almost as if an angel from heaven had reached down to bless me.

A GENUINE QUESTION

"Are we really going to New York?"

This was from a little girl at an English workshop entitled A Trip to New York. We certainly had pulled out all the stops to make her think so, even making her a little passport she had to produce, but alas, the trip was just a simulation.

CONVERSATION WITH A CHILD DURING A MISSION TRIP

Child: I've heard that there are gringos in your group.
Me: Yes. *I'm* one.
Child: Speak some gringo.

Children in Colombia often ask me to say something in English. So I do, and they laugh delightedly, as if I was speaking Martian.

FIRST-TIME FLYER

I am back from a weekend away at some friends' wedding. On one of the flights I sat beside a delightful four-year-old, flying for the first time, and full of questions:

"Why is it raining?"
"Why does it get dark?"
"Why is the seatbelt like this?"
"Are we going to fall?"

When we were airborne, he peeked out of the window and saw the lights of Bogotá below us.

"It's Christmas!" he exclaimed.

CONVERSATION WITH A CHILD

Me: What's that you've got there?
Girl: It's a little plum.
Me: I bet it's very sour.
Girl: Yes, delicious.

I don't get it! Colombians take a perfectly tasty fruit like an apple and put salt and lemon on it. Some even prefer green mangos to ripe ones.

CONVERSATION WITH A BOY

Me: What can I pray for you? What's your dream?
Boy: To go to school.
Me: How old are you?
Boy: Fifteen.
Me: Have you ever been to school?
Boy: No.

CONVERSATION WITH A CHILD

I met a child on the Seminary campus, a little girl who used to visit our office a lot. She ran up to me, gave me a big hug and said, "Have you found your Shrek yet?"

"No," I replied, sadly. "What am I going to do?"

"Don't worry," she said. "Your Shrek is going to come along and rescue you one day."

AC

I MET THIS LITTLE GIRL on the Coast.

You have the face of an angel.
You pout your little lips
to kiss me goodbye.
You put your little face
up to mine, trustingly,
a picture of innocence and love.
You live in a hut
the size of my kitchen.
The walls are made
from plastic sheeting.
There are little holes
in the corrugated iron roof.
The floor is pounded earth.

When it rains,
your house floods.
You probably don't know
your life is wretched.
But you will soon.

My Top Five Moments in Colombia (2008-2009)

My commitment to the Seminary was for two years and as time went on, I realized that I was finding life too difficult to think of staying for longer. Thankfully, I was able to meet with a wonderful former missionary and counsellor who "just happened" to be visiting the Seminary and after just two sessions the joy of my salvation was restored in a dramatic way. I was ready to consider extending my time there.

Towards the end of those first two years, I compiled the following list of my five top moments in Colombia:

5. ARRIVING IN SANTA ROSA

Santa Rosa is the community on the Coast where we built latrines last year. We were meant to have gone as a team to meet the people but things had gone horribly wrong earlier in the day. Two of the lads, including my co-leader Gabo, had hurt themselves falling off a motorbike, so in the end, I was despatched to make the first contact, along with Xiomara, the engineer from the NGO we were going to work with. The people were waiting to meet us and as we sat in the gloaming they told us about their lives, when they had been displaced and from where, how long it took to grow yucca and rice, how far their children had to go to school, how dirty the water was… I can't quite put my finger on why it was so lovely but maybe it was the location, nestling at the foot of wooded slopes, or the graciousness of the people, or my sense of God starting to put things together at the end of a traumatic day.

4. THE THANKSGIVING SERVICE IN SANTA ROSA

Five days later, Gabo, sufficiently recovered from his accident, preached at a little service we held to celebrate the end of our work in the community. The children (and adults) sat entranced as he preached on a passage in Luke 4:18-19: "The Spirit of the Lord is on me, because he has anointed me to proclaim good news to the poor. He has sent me to proclaim freedom for the prisoners and recovery of sight for the blind, to set the oppressed free, to proclaim the year of the Lord's favour."

It was a fitting ending to a wonderful week.

3. MY FIRST VISIT TO THE HOME OF A DISPLACED FAMILY

The first time I was invited to the home of a displaced family was during the mission in 2008 and I went with Gabo, since the women weren't allowed to go out on their own. In the dark, I hit my face on the barbed wire that marked the boundary of their plot but thankfully without much force. Yeffer, the 10-year-old son of the house, had invited us. His mum made us *avena*, a drink made from oats, and we sipped it down, trying not to think about how polluted the water was. From that simple act of hospitality and generosity out of extreme necessity grew a friendship that endured till I left Colombia and beyond.

2. MIDNIGHT FOOTBALL

I helped to distribute bread and hot chocolate in downtown Medellín. We had a lot of contact with a group of young adult men who live on the streets and are addicted to sniffing glue. For months they nagged us to bring along a football so they could play a match with the lads who came along to help give out the bread and chocolate. Finally, a ball was found and we picked a street for the match to take place in. Frankly, I didn't have high expectations for the game. The streets boys have an incredibly unhealthy lifestyle, and live in a context of extreme violence, so I felt the chances of a good, clean game of football were pretty low. Well, I couldn't have been more wrong. The game flowed from end to end, there was maybe one bad tackle in a couple of hours of play and you couldn't tell the street boys from the volunteers, either in terms of their fitness levels or their skills. The final score was something like 9-8 and it all ended in handshakes and hugs at about midnight. "This is the kingdom of God," I thought.

1. MIDNIGHT MEETING

Not only my top moment in Colombia until then but one of the most remarkable experiences of my life:

Again, the setting was downtown Medellín. I met a young man there in March 2009, at a particularly bad time for murders of street people. He told me he had come from Bogotá, that he was a drug addict and that he had studied theology in the past. All we did was chat to him and give him bread and jam, and hot chocolate. Months later, I was at a concert held in a church in the centre. A smartly-dressed young man came up to me and said in English, "Do you remember me?" It was the man I had met in March. We spoke briefly and made an arrangement to meet up the next day. He was living with his mother about 20 minutes from the Seminary. Over three or four hours I heard their story, with mother and son taking turns to tell their side. He said that that meeting had been a turning point for him – "It was as if you had given me the Holy Spirit with the bread and jam," he said. He was able to get back into contact with his family, find a church, go to a rehab centre, in short, to start again.

That Sunday, the day I heard his story, was my best day in Colombia.

The Middle

A Walk

AFTER TWO YEARS IN COLOMBIA teaching English in the Seminary, I spent almost a year and a half in Scotland preparing to return long-term. Not long before I went back, I spent some time on a retreat in the north of England, where I recorded the details of a walk I went on. It perfectly summed up the moment I was living.

The instructions are easy to follow.
First tarmac, then a green path.
'Not suitable for vehicles,' says the sign.
Hedgerows bridal white.
Primroses, violets.
Down rutted paths,
A ruined house.
The river, still as black glass.
Gorse reflected.
A fish leaps.
A set of concentric circles.

No compass required.
In the distance. Out of sight.
A waterfall.
My life.
At this precise moment.

I lay myself down

A SERIAL OVER-THINKER, I need moments of surrender, like this one I recorded on the same retreat in 2010.

Lord, I lay myself down.
Tired of trying to work it out by myself.
Of thinking, if I think
A little more, a little more deeply,
I'll get the answer,
And I'll be able to hold on to that answer
Instead of holding on to you.

El Salado and Ayapel

I RETURNED TO COLOMBIA in May 2011 to work with a project called Vive that was training churches to disciple children in areas affected by Colombia's long-running civil conflict. The first thing I did was to spend a month on a mission to a place called El Salado on the Atlantic Coast and helping a team that was bringing aid to communities devastated by flooding in another coastal area. These two contexts were the most extreme conditions I had experienced. The trip produced several blogs and some honest reflections.

BLOG: VILLAGE OF GHOSTS

This weekend I leave for a month-long trip to the Coast. With a team of about twenty people, I will be working in a village devastated by a terrible massacre about ten years ago. Initially, the inhabitants fled the area, but are now slowly returning. You might expect the words *love, peace, forgiveness* and *reconciliation* to ring hollow in a place of such horror, but actually, I expect to learn a lot about their true meaning there.

BLOG: CONVERSATION IN A BOOKSHOP

Me: Excuse me, I'm looking for the book about the massacre in El Salado.

Shop assistant: Let me go and see...

Two minutes later, shop assistant: I'm sorry, I have the book about the massacre in Trujillo and La Rochela but not El Salado.

BLOG: EL SALADO

The village I visited on the Coast, El Salado, has the same resonance in Colombia as Dunblane and Lockerbie in Scotland, that is, notorious for terrible acts of mass murder.

More than sixty people were murdered there over three days in February 2000. The massacre was carried out by paramilitary forces, with state collusion. Google it if you want to know more, but be warned, it's all pretty grisly. Colombian President, Juan Manuel Santos, visited El Salado three days after we left, and apologised for the massacre on behalf of the state.

Physically, the village is a shadow of its former prosperous self, but the people who live there are extraordinary: warm, open, generous and resilient. More than ever on this kind of trip, I went to bless, and ended up being blessed myself.

BLOG: EUPHEMISMS

Understandably, the people in El Salado don't tend to talk directly about the massacre, (although as we arrived, someone in the team overheard a child say: *We had a massacre and that's why*

43

people come to help us). They do talk about the displacement that followed, (and the 1997 displacement which preceded it), and they talk about the return, which happened two years later. If they need to talk about the massacre, they say *what happened to us*. I even heard someone call it *the accident*.

BLOG: FLOOD, PESTILENCE AND FAMINE

Not only did I get to know the wonderful people of El Salado on last month's trip to the Coast, but I got the chance to visit another part of Colombia, a part that was badly affected by flooding last year, and which is still under water.

I helped on a three-day Health Brigade. I swept up hair and treated children for lice, and thought about hunger.

BLOG: HUNGER

What does hunger look like?
Thin pigs.
Thin dogs.

I throw a dog some gristle, and a fleet-footed chicken snatches it from its mouth.

Fat children, with round, deceptive tummies, and blond hair, blond, through lack of protein.

And dull eyes.

BLOG: FLOODED LAND

1. Imagine…

a vast lake, a great inland sea. The only hints of something wrong are the tops of trees above the water, a constant hazard as we sail along.

2. I saw…
water lilies, stranded houses, a snake speeding away from the boat, a pair of sapphire dragonflies, entwined, an iguana splashing madly on the surface of the water.

3. These things happen…
We run aground, and the men have to get out and push the boat.
We crash into branches, and spend the rest of the voyage picking ants out of our clothes.
We hit a wasp's nest, and cannot blame the wasps for stinging us indignantly.
The man standing on the bow shouting directions falls in to the water, and his son cries with fright.

4. I think…
It's beautiful but deadly. Flooded land. Desperate farmers. A year without sowing, a year without reaping, a year without food.

BLOG: AID WORKERS

I am not an aid worker, but my experience on the Health Brigade got me thinking about what aid workers do:

We take photos of poor people with expensive cameras because our donors need pictures, and the more dramatic the better.

We eat better and more food in front of the hungry because there are lots of them, and not so many of us, and we need to be able to do our work.

We pour out our love to people displaced by the flooding, but next year, when the same people give up the struggle to live near their land, and arrive in the city to beg and to hustle for a living, it's possible that we will ignore them.

JOURNAL – BACK FROM THE MISSION

Of course, I loved it but it wasn't what I expected. I didn't see mass healings (ha ha!) or get weighed down by people's pain or act a great leader in the team. God made me smaller and smaller until what I was doing seemed virtually nothing at all. Cleaning a house, sweeping up hair, hugging a child.

But the memories are of the people: the warm, resilient people of El Salado and the hungry, grateful people of Ayapel.

Easter Sunday

A THOUSAND LITTLE DEATHS.
And the thousand and one times when I didn't manage to die
and I didn't even notice I was meant to.

 A thousand seeds sown.
Thousands of words.

How many will die on the rocks, snatched away?
How many will die in the earth and grown strong?
How much of a harvest to come?
No way to know.

A thousand dreams – and one sure hope:
that Sunday's coming.

Why I love Colombia

IN NOVEMBER 2011 after a trip to the Coast, I blogged:

Every missionary loves the country or people he or she has been sent to, that's surely a basic requirement, but when I am tootling along a leafy country road on the Coast, I can only praise God that I was given Colombia. It's as if in answer to some long-forgotten prayer, *Please don't let my life be boring,* I get to live in a in place that will provide enough need, beauty and excitement to last me as long as I live.

Despite (or perhaps, because of) the pain, violence and cruelty they have experienced for decades, Colombians have found a way of living with warm, playful grace that I quickly came to appreciate. I started an occasional feature on my blog called "Reasons I love Colombia" and here are 20:

1. IT TAKES A VILLAGE TO RAISE A CHILD

When a child gets on a bus, everyone takes responsibility for his or her well-being. Hands reach out to pass him or her safely up the aisle to a seat; nobody would dream of taking offence at all these strangers touching their child.

2. DANCE LIKE NO ONE IS WATCHING

I am in a taxi, careering down a hill. For a split second, I catch a glimpse of a security guard moving across the courtyard of an educational establishment. Not walking, but shimmying; doing a nifty little dance move.

Just for the fun of it.

3. DENIED A VISA? WRITE A SONG ABOUT IT!

One of my Colombian friends, a talented singer-songwriter, applied for a visa to the United States. He was turned down. His response? To write a song. A witty, light-hearted, non-bitter, faith-filled song about the experience, complete with audience participation.

4. LIVE MUSIC IN SUPERMARKETS

Admittedly, not every day, but during the recent Festival of Flowers, there was a little band playing in my local supermarket.

5. SUCH EASY GRACE!

I witnessed a tiny interaction in the metro the other day, and it seemed to sum up so much of what I love about Colombia. The metro is policed in part by young lads doing their national service and one of these was assisting a very frail old lady. First, he waited with her while her daughter went to get the tickets. He cupped his hand over her wrinkly forearm, and when it was time for her to go through the turnstile, he gently steered her through.

6. LOST PROPERTY

The Medellín Metro is running a campaign to highlight their lost property office and this is how they are doing it:

Strewn around the central station are oversized versions of articles you might lose while travelling. So far I've spotted outsize spectacles and a massive purse (to give you some idea, they are bigger than the size of a shopping trolley). I like this not so much because someone had a good idea (there are creative people everywhere) nor that such a thing could be produced (this is a huge city which provides every imaginable service) but the fact that the metro has a budget for this sort of playfulness, when a poster would have done a similarly effective job.

7. MUSIC

Everywhere.

8. THE WAY RANDOM PEOPLE REMEMBER ME

Example:

I live in a residential complex that has a gym but no shop. The complex next door has a shop and one day I went to buy something there. I also have friends who live further up the hill so when I walk up to visit them, I always pass the neighbouring complex. Now the security guard, who, remember, had seen me ONCE, always greets me like a long lost friend.

9. SERVICE

When you ask where you can find something in a shop, the assistant will accompany you to the right place.

10. COURTESY

Colombians in general, and Paisas (that's people from Medellín and the surrounding area) in particular, are just *so* polite.

In a supermarket, at the motorway toll, on the street, the most inconsequential interaction is transformed by the rituals of greeting and farewell. At the end of a flight I took recently my neighbour, an older lady, turned to me and said, *"Ha sido un verdadero gusto compartir este vuelo con Usted."* (It has been a real pleasure to share this flight with you).

I mean to say, has that sentence ever been uttered (without irony) in English?

11. BIO-DIVERSITY

Colombia has 0.66% of the world's population, 0.007% of the world's landmass, and a staggering 10% of the world's plant species. The practical consequence of such prolific life is that there is always something new to see: trees in flower, flowers in bloom, an orange, black and white butterfly that flits across my path, a bug that looks exactly like a moving segment of orange, a bumble moth...

12. POETS ARE HONOURED

An elderly poet makes the semi-final of Colombia's Got Talent. Emotionally declaiming his poetry, he wowed the crowd and every verse was cheered to the rafters.

13. EMPANADAS

Is there anything more delicious than these crispy meat pancakes, drenched in guacamole?

14. RUSH HOUR ON THE METRO

We are crammed in to the carriages. I am regretting having bought strawberries before getting on as they are in danger of being pureed before I get home. Uncomplainingly, the travellers adjust to allow the tide of newcomers at every station to find a space. When I get off, a man who gets off with me shouts, "Look, there's loads of space in the middle of the carriage, just budge up a bit!"

Of course there wasn't, so everybody laughed.

15. IF SOMETHING FUNNY HAPPENS, PEOPLE LAUGH

Sometimes that laughter can have a tinge of cruelty in it, but often it is just a laugh of pure amusement at the absurdity and comedy of life. Last week I passed a man sitting on a chair on the pavement outside a barber's. He moved his feet just as I came up parallel with him so I thought he was going to trip me up. I did a nifty little shuffle to avoid him, and caught the eye of a lad watching.

We both laughed.

16. A GENTLEMAN WITH A DIRTY FACE

I am walking down the hill to work on recycling day. Medellín's army of recyclers strips our rubbish of anything of value like a horde of human locusts. At one point, the rubbish has spread over the pavement and I step off on to the road to pass by. In a flash, one of the men picks up the rubbish and gestures with a courtly flourish for me to continue on the pavement.

17. GOD AT THE CENTRE

Here, God has not been pushed to the margins of public life. An example: There is a talent show for children on TV just now, called *Factor XS* (the S stands for Small). A child is asked if he thinks he will advance to the next round. "It's in God's hands," he answers simply.

18. I FIT RIGHT IN!

I don't turn heads. No one stares at me. I have dark hair. I don't have dark eyes, but I look into eyes like mine often enough, especially here in Medellín. Unfortunately, as soon as I open my mouth, it's a different story.

19. LET'S MAKE IT WORK

When I go to work I carry my rucksack on my back and my lunch in a plastic bag. One day I got on the bus, and realized would have to stand for the short journey down the hill. In the process of finding a place to stand, I first biffed a young man in the face with the rucksack; he smiled pleasantly and said, "*Tranquila*," (don't worry). Then a lady sitting behind him reached over and took my plastic bag, so that I had both hands free to hold on (for grim life).

A thousand small courtesies like these make Colombia a very special place.

20. HAMMOCKS

Peru

I WAS BORN IN PERU to Scottish parents and I ended up in Colombia by mistake. At one stage in my life, I thought it was very likely that I would end up as a missionary in Peru, but God had other plans. Once in Colombia I picked up eucalyptus leaves and their scent transported me back to childhood picnics under the eucalyptus trees outside Cajamarca, the town in northern Peru where I grew up and where I lived until I was almost eight years old. There and then I wrote "Eucalyptus", probably the only true poem I have ever written.

Eucalyptus

I found a spring of eucalyptus
on the path.
I picked it up
and bruised the leaf,
Released the tang of picnics long ago.
The hard-boiled eggs,

The melamine,
The tartan rugs,
And AA Milne.
That green-eyed child,
Could not know then,
What I know now:
The scent lies in the bruising.

Third Culture Kid

SEVERAL YEARS LATER, I got the opportunity to visit Peru for the first time in over 30 years. While I was there, I wrote a very mundane diary, recording where we went, who was there and what we ate (important in Peru, where the first question the taxi drivers ask you is, "What do you think of the food here?") But when I visited Cajamarca, I experienced that overwhelming internal pressure that says, "I have to write something about this feeling". The following two pieces were the product of that feeling:

I was born in Lima, Peru, and when people ask why, I say that it was where my mother was at the time, and they laugh, which is the idea. The reason my mum was there was that she had gone to Peru to be a missionary (with my dad), and she was learning Spanish in Lima when I arrived. Three months later we went to live in Cajamarca, a town in the northern part of Peru, and, apart from nine months in Scotland when I was three, I lived there until I was seven, nearly eight.

We left Peru, partly because my parents were concerned about my schooling and didn't want to send me away to boarding school. When I was told we were leaving, I cried a great torrent of tears. I lay on the wooden floor of my bedroom and kicked my feet and sobbed, "Mi Perú, mi Perú", and "Collie, Collie" (our dog). My toys were given away ("Think how much the children in the children's home will like playing with your dolls' house," my mother said), goodbyes were said and we left early in 1977. We arrived in Scotland in January. "Why is the sky all chugged up?" I complained, missing the clear blue Andean skies. Slowly I began the process of adapting to my new environment. My English accent, picked up from my expatriate playmates, had to go pretty quickly, and it did. I probably shouldn't have bragged that I had eaten guinea pig, a Peruvian delicacy, a stigma that followed me through my school years. I did ok as a child, less well as a teenager, then found a wonderful group of university friends, my friends to this day, who accepted me as I was, guinea-pig-eater and all.

In time, Peru became something mythical, almost legendary. My childhood remained frozen in the black and white photos I pored over and the memories that I would occasionally bring out to retell, thus ensuring their endurance in my mind. I forgot my Spanish almost immediately and only learned it again as an older teenager. I was terribly conflicted when Scotland played Peru in the 1978 World Cup, a dilemma I resolved by making the flags of both countries to wave (Peru won 3-1).

I grew up, I travelled, I befriended strangers, I tended to be friends with people with similar experiences to mine, I felt like an outsider everywhere, and yet I fitted in easily everywhere, too. I rejected the tag third culture kid until I read a book that exactly described my experience and I reluctantly accepted my status. I

58

came to see my childhood as a blessing, not a curse, an experience that gave me perspective, that allowed me to be a writer of sorts, that helped me relate easily to people from other cultures.

But for decades, I did not return to Peru.

And then in 2004 I saw the film *The Motorcycle Diaries* and thought, "Now it's time to go back," and I planned my journey, originally to both Colombia and Peru, but something – time? money? stopped me getting to Peru, and I was beguiled by Colombia, with its infinitely complex story and terrible pain, and that is where I stayed, until a Scottish friend, currently living and working in Lima, invited me to stay. After a couple of days in Lima we headed to Cajamarca to start our holiday proper.

The first night in Cajamarca I cried myself to sleep: little was familiar and I couldn't decide if what I recognized was from photos or from my memory. I knew there was no way to know. The buildings looked back at me, dumbly. I had left no mark here, there was no blond seven-year-old child waiting for me to explain it all.

The next few days I spent outside Cajamarca, having the kind of great holiday for which Peru is justifiably famous.

When I came back I started to make contact with friends of my parents – some providentially on holiday in the area, and little by little my frozen past thawed. People who had only been names or dimly remembered, stepped forward to say, "We remember you, we remember your parents." One family had photos of me as a baby, one taken with the grandfather of the family, and others remembered babysitting me. (Most of the members of a numerous family seemed to have cared for me at some point.) Another visitor, someone I had actually met in the intervening years was there to greet me, warmly.

Why the warmth? We do not know each other now, and yet our shared past is enough.

The mythic past became an everyday reality but it is better so. The faces in the pictures have become real people and by the wonders of technology and the casual intimacy of Facebook we can stay in touch, follow each others' ups and downs and be connected again, after all those decades of silence.

Why did this trip mean so much to me, so much so that I spent much of it near to tears? Because it means that my life starts at the beginning, that those first eight years mattered, and not just to me. It means that I didn't imagine or invent it all and that that part of my life which died, and it was a real death, can be resurrected to a new set of relationships and a new set of connections.

I am a Third Culture Kid. I belong everywhere and nowhere, and that's OK.

People and places

A PLACE IS NOT A PERSON.
But it should be.
"You spent your childhood here?
Welcome!
Here is bread and salt. A garland.
Take my hand, I'll show you
the slope you rolled down
and broke your arm,
(a green-stick baby break).
The cloth you spilled the milk on.
The wall you bounced a ball on.
The road to school.
I remember you. You belonged here.
You belong here."
But a place is not a person.
People can say,
"You were blond when you were small.

Look, a picture of you with our grandfather.
I remember you ran away.
Your house, your school,
your baby sitters.
Your mum, your dad.
We loved you then,
we love you now."

Lists

I LOVED MAKING lists of things, things I'd seen, learned, and done. A list made for a good blog post or a neat paragraph in a prayer letter.

A LIST OF THINGS I LEARNED DURING MY FIRST MONTH ON THE COAST

1. Mixing cement is like making a cake.
2. Laying bricks is like icing a cake.
3. Some things get so dirty they will never be clean again.
4. I can survive on five and a half hours sleep.
5. In the case of a flood, it's important to locate your toilet paper.
6. If you decide to share, you will always have more than enough.
7. The Spanish words for *lice*, *dandruff*, *stitch*, *bat*, and *bobble*.
8. A well has to be dug more than 100 metres away from a septic tank.

9. A flushing toilet is a wonderful thing.

10. You have to lie at an angle to sleep comfortably in a hammock.

A LIST OF THINGS I DID ON THE MISSION TRIP TO EL SALADO

1. Cleaned up puppy vomit (twice).
2. Helped to dig a hole.
3. Swept up freshly cut hair.
4. Treated children for lice.
5. Told a taxi driver how I became a Christian.
6. Helped to paint a joist with anti-rust paint.
7. Encouraged a group of women to build their lives on Jesus.
8. Picked up litter.
9. Blew up balloons.
10. Handed out flyers.

TEN THINGS I NOW KNOW ABOUT ORCHIDS THAT I DIDN'T KNOW ON SATURDAY MORNING

(This was after I'd done a course at the Botanic Gardens in Medellín. I came home bursting with knowledge and proceeded to kill off all my orchids).

1. Vanilla is derived from a species of orchid.
2. Orchid pollen is not carried on the wind but by insects.
3. Some orchids produce a scent reminiscent of the female of the insect that pollinates it.
4. Many species of orchids are epiphytes, that is, they grow on trees.
5. Orchids are not parasites.
6. Orchids always need to drain when they are watered.

7. The national flower of Colombia is the orchid *cattleya trianae*.

8. Orchids need to be fed with a mixture of potassium, nitrogen and phosphorus.

9. You should always sterilize your secateurs before cutting an orchid.

10. I have been mistreating my orchids very badly.

MY TEN MOST MEMORABLE MOMENTS OF 2016

1. Crossing the Minch for the first time.

2. Watching a ship going through the Panama Canal.

3. Shaking hands with Samuel Escobar (an eminent Latin American theologian) in the queue for breakfast at a conference.

4. Listening to a US man telling me about his legal marihuana-growing business, over lunch in my church in Colombia.

5. Finding a young woman unconscious on the pavement on my way to work.

6. Discovering Romans 5:17.

7. Spotting a scorpion crawling out of my flatmate's bedroom.

8. Witnessing two American (I mean US) men brawling on a flight in Colombia. The Colombians booed and jeered and the woman beside me said, "Gringo, go home." One brave Colombian stood between them.

9. Seeing the oldest evidence of Christianity in Scotland. (The Latinus Stone, from ca. 450AD).

10. A frosty day out in Ulm, Germany, with an old friend.

THINGS I'VE SEEN ON THE MEDELLÍN METRO RECENTLY

1. A male ballet dancer, holding on to the metal bar, doing his exercises.
2. A woman making an origami swan.
3. Someone reading her Bible.
4. Someone painting her nails.
5. And several examples of "cultura metro" in action, people leaping up to let the elderly, the pregnant, children and the injured have a seat.

SEVEN THINGS I SAW ON MY WAY TO WORK THIS MORNING

1. A huge, dead rat on the street down from my flat.
2. A man on a bicycle, hitting a submerged pothole and going straight over the handlebars into a puddle of dirty water.
3. An old woman picking out food from a rubbish bin and storing it carefully in a plastic bag.
4. The bus driver spitting out the window.
5. A man playing a marimba.
6. Neatly dressed Jehovah's Witnesses beside their stand of literature.
7. The street cleaner at the bottom of my street. I sure hope he got to the rat.

FIVE THINGS I SAW TODAY

1. Vehicles from the United Nations mission monitoring the peace process.

2. About 10 policemen guarding a supermarket entrance. A woman and a boy came out with their shopping and were hustled into a police car.

3. A shopkeeper throwing a bucket of water over a drunk man sleeping on the pavement.

4. A man injecting himself in the stomach.

5. A security guard walking down the street making a balloon animal.

TEN THINGS I LOVE ABOUT MY CHURCH

1. There are very old people
2. And babies.
3. There are people with learning difficulties.
4. There are black people
5. And white people.
6. Everybody knows my name
7. And is interested in my work.
8. We sing the doxology every Sunday.
9. People love Jesus.
10. Lunch there costs less than a pound (just over a dollar).

SEVEN THINGS I SAW TODAY (IN CHRONOLOGICAL ORDER)

1. A woman doing her make-up as she drove down the hill outside my flat.

2. A motorcyclist lying motionless on the road.

3. The cutest little girl solemnly waving goodbye to everyone as her mum carried her off the bus.

4. Two men siphoning petrol from a motorbike.

5. Four blond foreigners on the metro.

6. A young man delicately rummaging through a rubbish bin.

7. Two men pushing a car up the slope outside my house

FIVE THINGS I SAW THIS WEEK

1. A man with odd shoes on: one white, one black.
2. A man sleeping on the pavement with one shoe on and one bare foot.
3. A prostitute with the face of an angel.
4. Some little male football players trying to get their female coach's ear-studs back in (on the metro).
5. And a duo whose act at the traffic lights included heading a ball back and forward while juggling.

MY TRIP TO THE COAST IN BITES

Mosquitos: 100+
Insect that lives in the grass and leaves a little red mark in the centre of the bite: about 5
Jelly fish: 3
Wasps: 2
Ants: 1
Dogs: 0
Children: 0
Snakes: 0

The Story of Vive

IN 2017 I USED MY BLOG to tell the story of Vive, one instalment a day for a month. I did it as a fundraiser, and in fact, I did raise a little money through the initiative, but the main benefit was creating a record of the first few years of Vive's existence before many of the principal players moved on.

On one level, Vive's story begins in 2002 with the arrival in Medellín of our founder, Latin Link missionary Simon Walsh, to teach in the Bible Seminary of Colombia. The following year, he began taking groups of Seminary students on short-term mission trips to areas affected by violence and displacement on Colombia's Caribbean Coast. And what he found were communities full of children, hundreds and hundreds of children. Around the same time, a teenager called Leonardo Ramírez from the Colombian city of Bucaramanga was preparing to go to the Seminary. Leo's vocation was to work with children. And me? I was back in Edinburgh after having worked for three years in

Germany, convinced I was going to make a career in academia and NEVER go anywhere ever again.

Communities full of children, local churches, a visionary leader and Seminary students eager to serve in a part of their country badly affected by the conflict: all key elements of the early years of the Vive story. What was missing? A circus tent, of course! In 2005 Simon was able to buy one. In it thousands of children have since heard the good news of salvation in Jesus presented in an accessible way. Displaced adults have sheltered in it; it was used in the relief effort in Mocoa (a city in southern Colombia devastated by a landslide in April 2017); nights of peace and reconciliation have been held in it and I once helped to wash it.

The same year as the tent was acquired, 2005, the name *Funky Frog* (in Spanish: *Rana Bacana*) was given to the ministry. Funky Frog sounds good in English but Rana Bacana positively trips off the tongue in Spanish. Try it (making sure to roll the opening *r*). The name actually comes from a catchy children's song, but the idea was inspired, allowing a distinctive image to be established that was soon widely recognised. With his typical hat and shirt, the funky frog is instantly recognisable as being from the Coast or *costeño,* something local, not imported.

While all this was happening in Colombia, I was discovering that I didn't like academia as much as I expected, and experiencing that strange restlessness that sometimes comes before a radical change. Eighteen months later, I started teaching in the Seminary (Leo was one of my first students) and six months after that, I visited Colombia's Atlantic Coast for the first time, on one of the those short-term mission trips. But even then, if you'd told me I was going to end up working with *Rana Bacana* I wouldn't have believed you.

In 2008, while I was teaching English in the Seminary in Medellín, I went on a month-long mission trip (with Simon and Leo, among others) to Colombia's Atlantic Coast, an area of the country that has suffered deeply in the decades of civil conflict. It was the first time that I had been confronted with the scale and impact of forced displacement: hundreds of hungry, desperate (and welcoming) people living in tiny shacks. For the first time, the displaced had names and stories to tell.

In the first place we worked in, the circus tent again played its part by hosting events for children and adults, but as it happened, I opted out of helping with the Funky Frog event for the local children (too much jumping around in the searing heat for my liking!) and I found my niche treating children for lice. The trip made a huge impact on me and sowed the seed for my later involvement with the Vive Foundation and the Funky Frog Clubs, both a mere twinkle in their founder's eye.

In 2009 the Funky Frog team designed a Diploma for churches on how to work with children at risk, including a module on how to set up a children's club, and taught it over several months in two places on the Coast. It seemed to be a fantastic success: about 700 people signed up and there was a great buzz about the whole thing. It was only afterwards that it became obvious that only about 20 children's clubs had been formed in the wake of the event, and hardly any of those survived longer than a year and a half. This experience was very significant for the later development of the Funky Frog Clubs because it showed that from-the-front "training" didn't make change happen. There had to be another way and in 2010, Simon and Leo found it. The other unexpected consequence of the Diploma was that the Funky Frog now had hundreds of friends all over the Coast, people who were happy to host us and to spread the word when the Funky Frog came to town.

After the apparent failure of the diploma, it was time to look for a new approach. From the experiences of the previous years a couple of things were becoming obvious:

1. RELATIONSHIPS ARE KEY

Both the relationship between children and their Sunday School teachers, (or their leader-friends, as they became known), and between the Funky Frog team and the churches. Instead of training events with hundreds of participants, the strategy became encounters with groups of ten to 20 leaders in which real relationships could be built.

2. LEARNING BY DOING

For real change to be effected, the leaders needed to try the activities out, reflect on their experiences and then try them again. All this reflection came together in what became the first Funky Frog Club (given the name "The Milk and Honey Club"), in the town of Sahagún on the Caribbean Coast. Supported by the local pastor and his family (dear and loyal friends to this day) and the leadership of his denomination, Leo and Simon worked for months with the church's children's ministry to come up with the elements which became central to all the Funky Frog Clubs: play, worship, Bible teaching and prayer, all in the context of warm, loving relationships. In short, making children into disciples of Jesus.

A key part of the Funky Frog Club is the games afternoon (called the Extreme Afternoon or *Tarde Extrema* in Spanish) in which the leaders play alongside the children, preferably games that are energetic and entertaining. The Extreme Afternoon also has space for other activities, like science experiments, kite-making/flying and art projects.

Why play? You may not have reflected about the importance of play in your childhood but imagine what your life as a child would have been like if you had rarely played and if you had never played alongside adults. In fact, the games afternoon is the perfect place to build the relationships on which all the activities of the Club depend. In one place, the leaders instituted a small addition to the activity, gathering the children in small groups after the games and asking for their prayer requests, an innovation which became part of the training for new Clubs. Somewhere else, the concept of play was so novel that the leaders took time out of the training weekend to play by themselves. They had never played in their lives!

The Extreme Afternoon is a key element of a Funky Frog Club but of course, there's more.

On Sundays there is the Sunday Meeting (not School!) in which the leaders and children worship God together (this part is called *Todos Adorando* or Everybody worshipping). They then divide into three groups (for children aged three to five, six to eight and nine to eleven) to learn the Bible (called *Caminando con Jesús* or Walking with Jesus). And how do they learn the Bible? By following the Funky Frog curriculum, of course! The final and crucial activity of a Funky Frog Club is the Leaders' Prayer Meeting in which the leaders pray for each other, for the activities of the Club and for the children's needs.

Think about all this commitment for a moment: Running around in the blazing heat for a couple of hours on a Saturday, participating in the worship and teaching time on a Sunday, the hour of prayer, possibly on another week night PLUS any preparation required for the Sunday lesson…being a Funky Frog Club leader is a serious thing. But then, our Funky Frog Club leaders are seriously committed! After the first Club was established and the Club's activities defined, the next step was to start three more pilot projects in churches on the Coast.

As the first Funky Frog Clubs were established, it became clear that the leaders could use on-going training and support both to expand their knowledge and skills but also to encourage them to persevere in their work with the children. The idea of an annual camp for the leaders was mooted and the first camps were held in 2013. At first there were two, then three and now there are four, held in all the areas where we have clusters of Clubs. In addition, a training event in the circus tent is held once a year, at which representatives from all the Clubs learn how to run a camp for their children and practise the activities with local children.

While all this early development was happening, I was back in Scotland having completed my two-year commitment to the Seminary, convinced I would return to Colombia one day but not quite sure as to what my role there should be. It was at this point that Simon got in touch to ask if I would consider managing the development of a curriculum for the Bible teaching segment of the Sunday meetings in the Funky Frog Clubs and I said yes. (This is a very simplified version of what felt like a very drawn-out 16-month process!) I arrived back in Colombia in May 2011 and after the month's mission trip, I started work in what we were then calling Vive Kids. My first task was to visit the existing Clubs to get a feel for the project.

Now there are over 50 Funky Frog Clubs (in June 2020), not including what we call "Pirate Clubs", Clubs run by leaders who have learned the model informally from an official Funky Frog Club nearby (every so often the Pirate Clubs are "demobilized", receive the official training and formally become part of the programme). Most Clubs are on the Coast but we are experimenting with the model in Medellín and dozens of churches and schools around the country use our Bible curriculum.

My task for my first few years in Vive was to manage the development of the curriculum for the teaching slot in the Sunday meeting. The challenge was to tell the story of the Bible in six episodes (*Creation, Fall, Israel, Jesus, the Church* and *New Creation*) in a year. Which stories to tell, which to leave out, which to tell every year, which only once, how to recruit and train writers, and how to link the stories together with some sort of narrative thread, these were the questions that preoccupied me all the time I was in charge. Now my successor and former neighbour in the office, María del Mar, has to wrestle with them!

Probably no task of my life has stretched me more but how satisfying when the leaders started reporting that the children were enjoying their classes as never before and responding to what they were learning.

At the first camps, in 2013, we included some training on the prevention of sexual abuse. Reflecting on the response to that training we realized various things:

1. We needed to keep training ourselves in this area.
2. We needed to focus on prevention, first.
3. Many leaders had themselves been victims of abuse.

I started reading around the issue and last year did some online training, offered by an amazing Argentinian ministry that works in this area. In 2014, we were able to acquire some materials that had been produced in Peru to teach children how to protect themselves from abuse and we adapted them for our Clubs. Now, every child in a Funky Frog Club has received a nine-week course in how to identify and avoid risky situations (called Happy, Healthy Lives). We later developed a course on how to be safe online. As for helping the leaders, we have managed in a very small way to get professional help for them, but often all we have been able to do is listen when someone tells their story (which often begins "I've never told anyone this before…").

What has been the impact after all this effort? Although much of the work goes on beyond our sight, enough stories of transformation reach us to keep us going:

The little boy, traumatized and vengeful after the murder of his brother by an armed group who gave up his thoughts of revenge after some time in the Club.

The two brothers who recognised themselves in the story of the Jesus and the two blind men: "We're the beggars and you're Jesus," they said to their startled leader. On investigation, it turned out that the church has rebuilt these boys' house after it was destroyed in a storm.

The boy, on a local armed group's hit list because he was a thief, who probably had his life saved because his local Funky Frog took him in and turned his life around.

Of course, we set out in faith that our model would be transformative but what we didn't perhaps expect was the impact on the leaders. We quickly realized that in training and equipping children's club leaders on the Coast, we were unleashing huge potential. Even the local pastors commented on the change in the leaders' demeanour as they took on more responsibility and ownership of the project. I had my a-ha moment about this back in 2013 when I watched some of our leaders working with a group of boys at the first circus. The leaders were from an indigenous community (traditionally a very marginalized group) and the youngsters were from an extremely violent neighbourhood. They were the most aggressive children I've come across in Colombia and some of the other leaders had tried an authoritarian approach with them, which of course, hadn't been a great success. But these indigenous leaders were teaching the Bible story in their usual gentle way, without raising their voices or using any tricks, just depending on God and acting in a kind, loving way. The boys were transfixed! I realized then that these leaders, of no value to the world, were princes in the Kingdom of God, with or without the Vive Foundation, but Vive made it possible for me to witness their triumph and for you to know about it!

And that was how my online story of Vive ended but of course, that was not the end of the story of Vive. As I write, the work of training churches to disciple children in Colombia continues, and 720 leaders serve 3700 children in the 50 plus Funky Frog Clubs have. And we are still looking for funding! You can donate to the wonderful work of the Vive Foundation via Latin Link: https://www.latinlink.org.uk/appeal/vive-foundation.

A Movement not a Monument

APART FROM THE BLOGS on the story of Vive collected in the previous chapter, I only occasionally blogged about Vive but I almost always included something about our work in my prayer letters:

BLOG JULY 2011

I STARTED WORK!

I started work in my new project today. It's called *Vive* and its aim is to train churches in the poorest areas of Colombia to care for children in their communities. My role is to manage the curriculum development for all the areas of the project. The most exciting thing about it is that I have a little garden at the office which is mine to tend, so today I bought a trowel and a watering can. Tomorrow I plan to plant nasturtiums and deadhead the roses.

BLOG AUGUST 2011

A STRANGE AND HOLY GLEE

My work is challenging, frustrating, perplexing, daunting, impossible. But sometimes I am filled with a strange and holy glee when I remember that I am getting to be part of something SO HUGE.

PRAYER LETTER FEBRUARY 2012

I have compared my life in Colombia to a roller coaster before, but it is so true of our work at Vive Kids, developing resources for children's clubs in Colombia's poorest communities. One week, all is doom and gloom: the leaders of the pilot clubs are flagging; in one place the booklet with all the lessons has been lost; the children are being riotous (oh dear, was that our fault?!) Then, within a week, all is transformed: in one place the children are clamouring for their games afternoon to restart after the holidays, in two places the leaders' prayer meetings were especially blessed, a particular lesson worked well, and word comes of another child's life transformed.

BLOG MARCH 2012

AN ENCOURAGING WORD

A leader at one of the pilot children's clubs says, "Before you [the Vive team] came, we were working with the children with our fingernails. Now we are working with our hands."

PRAYER LETTER MAY 2012

VIVE

Working on the curriculum for the children's clubs is a bit like painting the Forth Road Bridge. As soon as we get one series of lessons finished, we celebrate for 10 minutes and then get started on the next one. But it's worth it. I visited two of the pilot clubs recently and it was wonderful to see the materials we toil over in the office being used, more or less successfully, with REAL children. Now we are working on the fourth series and revising the very first one.

BLOG AUGUST 2012

TREASURE IN JARS OF CLAY – OR IN BROWN PAPER PACKAGES?

This week we finished another series of lessons for the children's clubs on the Coast. We packaged them up and took them to the bus terminal to post them (Colombia's postal service is patchy, and the quickest way to send something is often on the regular bus services). The woman behind the counter asked what the packages were worth so as to include some insurance in the postage. We settled on $15,000 (about £5.20 or $8.20) which wouldn't even have covered the cost of the photocopying. But really, we should have said they were priceless. Not because they are anything special as lessons go, but because of the content: lessons on ways to live in harmony, to obey legitimate authorities, and on God's unfailing love and forgiveness.

Treasure indeed.

BLOG DECEMBER 2012

BEHIND THE CURTAIN

This has been an eventful year, with many, many challenges, but with many, many blessings: I kept well and safe. I travelled thousands of miles, without major incident. At work, we were able to produce 6 series of lessons for use by 7 children's clubs. How was that possible? Well, tonight I got a little glimpse behind the curtain, meeting with a group of people who have prayed for me every Wednesday for the last year and a half.

An unassuming little group, but full of spiritual warriors.

BLOG SEPTEMBER 2015

ALWAYS THE RIGHT ANSWER

Last weekend we travelled to quite a remote area on the Coast to hold a camp for our children's club leaders in that area. In fact, it was so remote, it was the end of the road. As someone told me, there was nothing else in one direction but the jungle and a few indigenous people.

About 70 leaders came to hear talks on The Lord's Prayer (have you ever thought what "Hallowed be your name" actually means?) as well as to receive training in activities they can implement with the children in their Club.

One of the activities was a "model lesson", in which I taught five adorable children aged four to ten one of our lessons while the 70 leaders took notes. I enjoyed it, although it did remind me of the dreaded "crit lesson" from my teaching training. The class ended with me asking the children what we could ask Jesus for and one of the four-year-olds, a little girl, looked at me with big, round eyes, and said, questioningly, "Amen?"

BLOG JANUARY 2017

A PRINCE

Imagine a little indigenous boy. First his mum dies, then his dad and his brother, leaving him alone in the world. He looks longingly through the windows of the houses of his community but people drive him away. Friendless and poor, life is a desperate struggle. Until, one day, the local church leaders take an interest in him. They let him live in the church, they share the love of Jesus with him, and little by little, he begins to understand the gospel. Psalm 65:4 becomes important to him: Blessed are those you choose and bring near to live in your courts! Fast forward to Saturday 7th January 2017. The boy is now a young man. He is dressed as a king. In fact, he is acting the part of the king in the Bible story of the unmerciful servant (Matthew 18:21-35) at the Vive Circus. He makes a good king, authoritative and then appropriately angry with the servant. The next day, children listen entranced as he tells his story and how he was able to forgive all the slights and hurts of his childhood and youth. Unassuming but confident, he is one of our local facilitators, and now considered a leader in his wider family.

"He [the LORD] raises the poor from the dust and lifts the needy from the ash heap; he seats them with princes, with the princes of his people," Psalm 113:7-8.

BLOG JUNE 2017

WHAT IT'S ALL ABOUT

Recently I visited a friend who had been one of the first children's club leaders ever trained by the Vive project. Over lunch, the lodger in the house quizzed me about the Vive Clubs. As I tried to explain what we are about, my friend chipped in, "To be a Funky Frog club leader is to become a child again. It's to get down to the level of the children and play with them as if you were a child yourself."

I couldn't have put it better myself.

BLOG SEPTEMBER 2017

FEEDBACK

On our camps we take some time to ask the leaders to evaluate our curriculum. We ask if anything significant has happened as a result of the lessons and here is what one leader told me last weekend. "The mum of one of the boys in the class came up to me and asked what we were teaching the children and when I asked why, she said, 'My little boy came home from his class and said, 'Mummy, read the Bible to me,' and when I asked why, he said, 'Because I want to be WISE.'"

BLOG SEPTEMBER 2017

RETURNING HOME

Last weekend I was away on one of the Funky Frog camps for leaders.

This weekend's camp was in an area called La Mojana, a region of outstanding natural beauty and biodiversity (one of the most bio-diverse areas in Colombia, which makes it one of the most bio-diverse on the planet). The theme was Returning Home, encouraging the leaders to experience and enjoy their relationship as sons and daughters (not servants!) in their heavenly Father's house. We also held workshops on keeping children safe on the internet, making resources out of easily obtained materials, being constructors of peace and working with children aged 9 to 11, the oldest children in the Club.

Apart from two huge thunderstorms with associated power cuts, all went well.

BLOG JANUARY 2018

THE HEART OF ART

Months and months ago, I sat poised over my keyboard, waiting for inspiration to strike. My task that day was to write a drama for children about the context of the giving of the 10 Commandments (we are nothing if not ambitious here at Vive!). The point of the drama was that the people of Israel were liberated from their oppression in Egypt before they were given the Law, a fact that the commandments themselves highlight. (Identity before behaviour is a key idea in the New Testament, too).

Anyway, I had the idea of an Israelite family talking about the Law and remembering the events of the Exodus while leafing through a family album of photos (anachronistic, I know). I imagined a family at one side of the stage and a huge "photo-frame" at the other, which would be uncovered now and then to reveal "frozen" actors, representing some part of the story (the oppression in Egypt, the Exodus, the first hard days in the desert). At one point, the actors would unfreeze and come out and act some more of the story. Fast-forward to today. I was scrolling through photos of this year's circus and there it was, the idea I had all those months ago, working, on the stage!

The Coast

ALL OF COLOMBIA *is fascinating but there is something special about the Atlantic Coast, the area between the end of the Andes range of mountains and the Caribbean Sea. For the first few years, the whole focus of Vive's work was in three or four areas of the Coast and I travelled there several times a year. There was always something extraordinary to see.*

COASTAL SNAPSHOTS

A little boy has made a simple kite from a stick and a plastic bag. He runs along with the stick above his head. The bag blows away but he runs on unaware.

"You've lost your kite," I shout as I tootle by on the back of a motorbike.

A little girl has made a kind of pet from an empty shampoo bottle and a piece of string. She drags it behind her into the shop.

I LOVE THE COAST

I love the Coast. Everyone is so relaxed, very different from up-and-at-it, go-ahead, money-conscious Medellín. And I have the feeling that anything could happen. Last week I saw three people on a motorbike (not unusual). A woman was driving. Next came a child. And finally, a man holding a floor fan. The wind was making the blades whirr so that for a moment, I wondered where the power source was.

Like I said, anything could happen on the Coast.

THE COAST WORKS ITS MAGIC

An unfortunate scheduling quirk meant I was off to the Coast a day after I arrived from Scotland. I spent the first couple of days in a jet-lagged daze wondering where I was, but the Coast was soon up to its beguiling ways again.

Life, colour, music and the zany were everywhere:

- a small, dull, grey butterfly turned out to have a row of peacock eyes down its wings
- a pig chased after a motorbike
- a little boy walked along a dusty street playing an accordion
- another beat out a rhythm on the hot plate of a fast food cart with a metal spike
- another carried an enormous yellow basin on his head.

LEAVING TOWN

The area I travelled to last week is pretty isolated. Public transport consists of a Toyota pick-up which makes two trips a day to several villages about an hour from the nearest town. There were five of us travelling and we were told there was only space in the back of the pick-up. Space we had to share with crates of tomatoes, bags of bottled water, crates of soft drinks, and many other sacks of things I couldn't identify.

Just when we were all settled, two more people were squeezed in and off we set.

Somehow there was something very amusing about the spectacle we presented, (the mattress strapped on the roof and the hula hoops we were taking for the children to play with may have been the cause) and a crowd gathered to cheer and holler as we rolled out of town.

Someone even took a picture of us on his mobile phone.

What I didn't include in my blog about this trip was that we shared the truck with a young lad with whom I chatted for a while, asking his name and where he was from. He seemed a bit reticent but I thought nothing of it until he got off and my travelling companions told me he was almost certainly a member of a paramilitary group which was why he didn't want to reveal much about himself.

RANDOM EXPERIENCE ON THE COAST

The pastor was peeling a big, green fruit. "This type of mango has a bit of a strange name," he said, with a twinkle in his eye,

"It's called horse buttocks. Have you ever seen such a thing in Medellín?

"Yes," I said, "but only on a horse."

THE SOUNDS OF THE COAST

Boom: a ripe mango falls on the corrugated iron roof of the house we are staying in. (But because, inexplicably, many Colombians prefer mangoes when they are green, many more fell, unripe, because they were prodded with poles).

Ca-chick-ca-chick: the *guacharaca*, a percussion instrument that looks for all the world like a cheese grater, and which provided the accompaniment to great, abandoned, full-throated worship of God.

Chugg-a-chugg-a: military helicopters overhead, an unwelcome reminder that the conflict wasn't far away.

Slosh-splash: the sound of people having showers by means of tipping buckets of water over themselves.

Oh, it was great. I had a lovely time.

THE COAST NEVER FAILS TO ASTOUND

I love Colombia because unexpected things happen all the time and on the Coast what happens is often particularly startling. At about 10 o'clock at night, I was sitting outside a house on the Coast with a group of friends waiting for pizza to arrive (this was to celebrate the birthday of one of the leaders and I hadn't known I was invited until we stopped outside her house and we all sat down).

Just then, a group of people came up the road including two men on stilts. We watched them stalk by in silence then returned to our conversation.

ALWAYS SOMETHING TO SEE

One of the great things about these trips to the Coast is that they give me loads of ideas for this blog! Just looking out of the window of the bus is entertaining. As we sped through a small town I caught a glimpse of a woman sitting on a chair holding a baby on her lap with one hand while cutting the grass beside her with a machete!

How's that for female multitasking?

THE COAST NEVER DISAPPOINTS

I had a quick visit to the Coast last weekend to do some training.

I was there for about 48 hours but of course there was fun stuff to see:

- a place called Bad Attitude Hill
- a lad opening a coconut with a machete
- an old woman with a bag of oranges on her head
- a T-shirt being worn by as upstanding a person as you could wish for with the words (in English): It feels so good to be bad.

THERE AND BACK AGAIN

Disappointingly, there were no motorbike rides during my latest trip to the Coast. Instead we got a minibus right to the entrance to the church where we were holding our first camp of the year for our children's club leaders. Over 50 came to receive training and teaching from the life of Paul.

On Saturday night, there was a huge thunderstorm which went on for hours. The rain hammering off the corrugated iron roof kept me awake until minutes before it was time to get up, or so it seemed, and the power was out until mid-morning. As I came to from my ten minutes of sleep, I heard someone singing, "I'm going to live this day as if it were my last." When I got up I saw the most amazing sunrise, a blaze of orange reflected in a lagoon, a sight so beautiful that I gasped. And I found everybody calmly getting on with their mornings, clearing up the mess caused by the storm, queuing for showers and waiting for breakfast. The ladies who were cooking for us had come barefoot through the mud because motorbikes couldn't handle the terrain. Everything started an hour late but nobody minded.

Welcome to the Colombian Coast, where nothing is ever a crisis.

CONTEXT IS ALL

Last weekend I was at a camp for our children's club leaders on the Coast in a town I usually associate with smothering heat. But God was gracious and it was relatively cool, allowing us to complete our activities with less sweat than usual. It was so cool for the locals that they sat shivering, huddled up in all the clothes they could find.

Would you like to guess what temperature it was? A chilly 26 degrees celsius. I told them that 26 degrees was a rare and roasting hot day in Scotland and they could hardly believe it!

THE COAST ENCHANTS AGAIN

I was on the Coast last week, literally, for a change (I got a wee dip in the Caribbean) and it was great fun, as usual.

It's just always so unexpected.

In the ladies' toilets at the airport in Montería, there was a workman perched on the toilet seat, working on the cistern and singing unselfconsciously along to his radio.

On the bus on the way to the town where our event was being held, there was a drunk man, and no seat for him so he held on to the bar, but occasionally one hand flopped down and patted me on the head. "Hold on with both hands," someone told him. Finally, a young country lad (complete with machete strapped to his thigh) let him have his seat where he promptly fell asleep.

And on the plane home, I listened in to a grandfather and grandson finding shapes in the clouds: "It's an elephant! No, a crocoelephant! No, a crocophelantceros! A car! No, a cake!"

In between we had a successful camp for 30 children's club leaders. The highlight of that was when two of them, older women who are neighbours, received a phone call to tell them that they were going to get materials to build a house. They actually jumped for joy!

The Song

I SPENT MUCH OF MY TIME in Colombia feeling overwhelmed, by the need, by the workload, by the heat, by my inadequacy, but just occasionally, I felt deep joy.

I am straining to hear the song.
I lean my ear into the wind
to catch the faintest echo
of the bubbling joy
in the Father's heart.

Tales from my Little Green Case

I HAD THE IDEA of telling the stories of my travels through blogs in the voice of my little green case.

FEBRUARY 2013

I love it when we go to the Coast. I get out and about so much. This time I had several rides on a motorbike, propped up in front of the driver. I was going to spend one journey lashed to the roof of the taxi but they didn't make a good job of that and I fell off after the first 30 seconds. I am pretty sturdy though, and there wasn't any harm done. They did a better job the second time and we got to Sincelejo in one piece. My favourite journey was in the back of a truck, safely tucked up in a stack of plastic chairs, like being in a little nest.

FEBRUARY 2013

The only thing I don't like is that she fills me so full. I thought my record was the first mission we went on in 2008: she got everything in that she needed for a month, including a hammock and wellington boots, but this time was pretty close. It was that blanket she needs for the bus that nearly broke my zip. But I am nothing if not expandable and she got me shut every time.

She boasts about me you know, says I am a magic case, that there is always space for one more thing. It's true really. Now I am back in Medellín, shut up in that big black case that got to go to Scotland with her. It's a bit dull after the Coast but I know it won't be long before she'll be hauling me out and stuffing me full again.

APRIL 2013

I wish she would make up her mind: first the hammock and the ropes go in, then the ropes come out, and finally, the hammock comes out. Her lovely big *sombrero vueltiao* goes in [the typical Colombian straw hat], only to be replaced by that shabby thing she bought in France. And finally, I don't get to travel in the plane with her after all, but get stuck in the hold. I bet I wouldn't have bounced about so much if I had been riding up top, snugly tucked into an overhead locker. Anyway, we made it here OK and that's the main thing. I'm looking forward to the next few days. I'm sure there will be a motorbike ride in there somewhere.

JUNE 2013

Well, this is all very strange.

Tomorrow I am going to be wrapped up in a black bag and sent off to Sincelejo BY MYSELF, (if you don't count some rather dull boxes, which I don't.) Of course, it's not the first time I have travelled by myself. Once, I got sent (by mistake) to Bogotá from Miami, and had to stay the night in a room with all the other misplaced cases, until she caught up with me. Anyway, it's an adventure, and I am not complaining. We should be reunited on Monday, all being well. Meanwhile, she's offering my space to all and sundry. All because someone or something called *Viva Colombia* [a low-cost airline] has a very limited baggage allowance.

JULY 2013

Grave news! A small tear has been discovered in one of my seams. Is this the end of the road? Am I now condemned to a lifetime as a storage facility? No more adventures? No more rides on motorbikes and on top of taxis? But there is hope. I heard her asking a friend where she could get me repaired, and I am sitting in the living room, not stored away, as if she hasn't given up on me, so I am trying to bear up as best I can.

JULY 2013

Good news! I've been fixed. It was a big adventure, as so much is here, that included narrowly avoiding big protest marches in the centre of Medellín, a cockroach climbing out of a cash machine, and a long taxi ride (I could see her calculating when it was going to be cheaper to buy a new case) but I finally got fixed for the princely sum of $5000, less than £2.

So I am ready for my next outing, and it's an exciting one but she says I can't tell you about it until we're back.

AUGUST 2013

So we set off from Medellín to Lima via Bogotá. We left on one of Colombia's Independence Days (yes, they have two), which meant the airport in Bogotá was closed for four hours for a flypast by the Colombian Air Force, but we made it to Lima eventually. After a weekend in Lima it was off to Cajamarca, and then over the Andes to Leymebamba and Chachapoyas on the most terrifying roads, winding in hairpins down hundreds of metres of steep slopes.

I was glad to be securely fashioned to the roof of the car, and if I had eyes, I would have shut them. Then it was back to Lima, via a few days in Cajamarca, and back to Medellín last Saturday. I am glad to report that my newly repaired stitching held. Now I am just waiting to hear when the next adventure is. I think it must be quite soon because she didn't pack me away in the big black case as she usually does.

It was all very exciting and emotional for her, because was born in Peru, you know, and she hadn't been back since she left aged seven and three quarters. No doubt she'll be emoting about it on these pages over the next few days.

JULY 2014

After what felt like months gathering dust under her bed, I finally got dragged out and was stuffed full (as usual) before we set off up the hill to the airport. Two flights, a bus ride and a trip in the back of a truck and we arrived somewhere cold and dark.

The next day, something we thought was a mobile phone woke us up, but it was actually a bird. I could see we were in a forest. She seemed to have a good time; she slept a lot, and disappeared every now and then, only to return all muddy, as if she had been for a walk.

It was called Ecuador, the place, I think.

And that was the end of stories from my little green case. It was brought to Scotland and now lives on top of the wardrobe, dreaming of past glories and no doubt annoying more recent arrivals with its traveller's tales.

On the buses

IT WAS ALWAYS AN ADVENTURE to get a bus in Colombia. On the short trip from my flat in Medellín to the nearest Metro Station or a ten-hour journey to the Atlantic Coast, there was always something of interest to see on the bus, or to be glimpsed through the window.

NEAR DEATH EXPERIENCE

The bus launches itself at the roundabout at exactly the same moment as a huge truck. A crash seems inevitable. The driver brakes sharply, sending us jerking forward. I clutch at the seat in front, and gasp with fright.

Nobody else reacts at all.

MIRACLE FLEET

One of the buses I get on belongs to the Miracle Fleet. As in, it's a miracle that you get off the bus alive.

HYPERBOLE

Another stressful bus ride today. The bus was so full that I got jammed in the door. I literally couldn't squeeze past all the people wedged on the bus to get off. A kind gentleman, who had got off to let me off, gave me his arm, and I finally popped out. "This is like being born," I gasped, melodramatically.

WHITE-KNUCKLE RIDE

I had THE MOST bone-shaking, nerve-jangling, teeth-rattling, hair-raising bus ride tonight. It was a new route for me and the baseball-capped driver jolted round corners, careered over potholes and sleeping policemen, stopped traffic to chat to another bus driver and tooted angrily when anybody else stopped him. I clung on to the seat in front and actually had red marks on the palms of my hands when I got off. What a relief to get into the calm order of the Metro.

THE BUS RIDE HOME

When it rains, as it did today, it gets very difficult to get a taxi home so when I saw there wasn't a long queue for the bus, I decided to join it and I didn't have too long to wait.

The peanut seller who works the bus queues said, "Oh, they've let you come to these parts again," and I said, "I usually get a taxi because it is such a pain to get the bus," and he said, "You're posh, you."

As it worked out, the bus wasn't too full for most of the 20-minute journey up the hill and then, two minutes from home, we stopped and an overfull bus in front off-loaded 10 to 15 passengers who all got on our bus. So when I had to get off, I had to force my way through a scrum of bodies; somebody got her long hair painfully yanked, toes were stood on, tummies squished. When I finally stood on the step, I turned back and said, a bit grandly, "I apologize to everybody I may have crushed," and some gracious people laughed.

When I got off the bus, my heart was pounding, I was short of breath, I was sweating – it felt like I had been at the gym.

Taxi tomorrow, I think.

BUS RIDE

Last Saturday I got caught in a traffic jam. A route that would take 10 to 15 minutes on a normal day, ended up taking an hour and a half. A combination of accidents and a holiday weekend conspired to make it a hot and frustrating journey. But as usual, the Colombians on board made the best of it. Some slept, some played games on their phones, and at the front, a group of older women befriended the bus driver, advised him on what to do and generally found the whole thing hilarious.

URBAN PROPHETS

Thousands of people make their living working on the buses here in Medellín, but there is one group that stands out for me.

They are young men that board the buses in the posher parts of town, sometimes singly, sometimes in pairs. They hold a little boom box under their arms to provide the rhythm, and they rap for a few minutes.

They rap about the social problems of the country, about injustice and violence, about corruption and inequality. I notice that people give generously to them, and I think it's because they are telling the truth, and because they have chosen a legitimate option to make money, out of the many darker avenues available to them.

WHY I ADMIRE BUS VENDORS

That's people who sell things on buses, not people who sell buses (who may be admirable, too, for all I know). People who sell things on buses in Medellín are incredibly agile, cheerful and stoic in the face of much rejection. First, they clamber over the turnstile because the driver is letting them ride for free. Then they deliver their sales pitch in a singsong chant (singsong from repeating it 100 times a day, I guess). The content of the chant is common to ALL vendors and goes something like this:

"First of all ladies and gentlemen, I wish you a pleasant morning/afternoon/evening. As you can observe, I am coming past each of your seats, offering you a delicious [type of product] called [name of product]. This product has the very economic cost of [price], and to save you money two [or three or four] for [discounted price]. Thank you and God bless you."

They then hand their product to everybody, receive payment from anybody who wants to buy, and collect what isn't bought, all the time balancing precariously as the bus careers along.

EXPERIENCE ON A BUS

A man gets on and greets the passengers, makes a critical comment about the money the US invests in Colombia, then explains that he is poor, that he lives by tutoring but that often there is only enough for one meal a day. His daughter is ill, and his health insurance provider is refusing to pay for the operation she needs. He is appealing the decision, but the case might take months to resolve, and meanwhile, could we help with a small donation? I am astonished to see that many people give him money, perhaps because most of them have been in a similar situation.

BUS BUSKERS

One day last week there was a musician performing on the bus going to work and a rapper (unusually for here, a young woman) on the bus going home. The musician was playing a wreck of a guitar but had a lovely voice, the rapper was slick, with hard-hitting lines about the reality of life here.

I thought, maybe one day this society will have progressed to the extent that young people can get the funding they need to study and won't need to busk in buses. But bus rides would get duller.

AN ANGEL WITH A BATTERED GUITAR

Last week an older man carrying an extremely battered guitar boarded the bus I was on, greeted us and began to sing. I have to say, I didn't have high expectations, but he had a remarkably tuneful voice and I almost immediately recognised the song, a setting of Psalm 37:4: Take delight in the LORD, and he will give you the desires of your heart. This was so perfect for what I was thinking and feeling that day, that I instantly felt utterly blessed and knew that God had sent this man onto that bus – which made him an angel, even if his guitar was a wreck.

QUID PRO QUO

A young man jumps on to the steps of the bus. He makes some kind of deal with the driver – who probably knows him – and he doesn't pay. At least not in money. He earns his passage to the bottom of the hill, by announcing our destination in ringing tones (imagine a British town crier) every time the bus stops.

CONVERSATION ON A BUS

A lad got on the bus and sat beside me.

This is some of the conversation we had:

Him: Could you spare me some change for some breakfast?

Me: Isn't there something else you could do? Like sell sweets?

Him: Later on that's what I'll do. But first, I have to get money for breakfast for my little brother and sister because there's no food in the house. [Before you read on, try and imagine that. Literally no food in your house.] Then I'll buy a box of chewing gum and go to work.

Me: How does that work out for you?

Him: It depends. Chewing gum is good. I pay $2,000 for the box and I can make $5,000 to $10,000 in day.

Me: What about your parents?

Him: My mum works as a housekeeper in another part of the city and I never knew my dad. My mum comes on Sundays. My little brother was injured in an accident to his spine and can't work. But he gets a pension. My little sister is doing well, she's in Primary 4. I studied to Primary 7 but I'm not studying now.

Me: And how old are you?

Him: 17.

TRANSCENDENCE ON A BUS

One day, a rapper got on our bus and said he was going to do something a bit different.

What he did was recite an old poem, a kind of melodramatic ballad about love, betrayal and death, over the backing of some classical piano music – maybe Chopin – that he had found on YouTube. The result was the most mesmerizing three-minute experience. The combination of words and music created a dramatic, tension-filled atmosphere and you could almost forget that you were jolting along on a bus.

Welcome to Colombia, where the hustlers on the buses are artists at heart.

Encounters with Colombians

I FOUND COLOMBIANS open, warm, witty and positive. The briefest conversation with a Colombian could make my day and still can.

CONVERSATION AT THE SEMINARY

Me: There is a dead bird in the chapel.

Student 1: Why didn't you give it mouth-to-mouth resuscitation?

Me: It was very dead.

Student 2: Why didn't you pray for it to be raised from the dead?

Me: I don't have enough faith for that.

COMPLIMENT (I THINK) FROM A STUDENT

"I understand most of what you say in class but I wouldn't if you weren't using your hands," says a student, talking about me using English most of the time in class.

A STUDENT, COMMENTING ON MY NEW HAIRCUT

"With you time goes backwards: you look younger as time passes."

COMPLIMENT FROM A COLOMBIAN (ONE OF MY COLLEAGUES)

"You've got *a little* rhythm."

MORNING CONVERSATION

Every morning I walk down the hill, I have this conversation with a man walking up:

Me: Good morning

The man: Good morning. All the very best! Have a good day!

Me: Thank you.

However much I try, I can never cram as much as he can into the three seconds we have as we pass each other by.

CONVERSATION ON THE PHONE, MID-JANUARY

Phone rings.

Me: Hello?

Older lady: Good evening. Is Don Rogelio there?

Me: No, I'm sorry, you've got a wrong number.

Older lady: Oh, I'm terribly sorry to disturb you, my dear.

Me: No problem.

Older lady: What a shame to make you answer the phone.

Me: It's no trouble.

Older lady: I must have the wrong number. I'll try again.

Me: Bye.

Older lady: Goodbye, goodbye. Happy New Year.

Only someone from Medellín could make such a social event out of a misplaced phone call.

MAN AT THE DOOR OF THE VIVE OFFICE

"I'm very sorry to bother you, I'm not asking for money, let me tell you what I am asking for. We've just arrived here from Honda, they've given us a little house in San Javier, thank God, but we need shoes, a little blanket, a pair of trousers, not all these things of course, look, I had to come out in a pair of my wife's trousers. Thank God, I'm not dirty. Or a pound of rice, a little pan. Or some money for some lemonade and some bread."

TOOT

Walking down the hill to work, I stumble over something, a wire, a strand of tough grass, I'm not sure what. It jerks me forward and I take a giant, comedy stride, before, thankfully, regaining my equilibrium, and continuing on my way. A taxi driver, coming up the hill toots his horn. I puzzle over that toot.

Did it mean: *Are you OK?*
Do you need a lift after getting that terrible fright?
I saw that?
Or even, *Ha ha!?*

LOST IN TRANSLATION

Just when I thought I had mastered traffic management (stopping a bus or taxi with a flick of a finger) I have had two recent mis-communications with taxis. Walking down the hill to catch my bus to work taxis often toot questioningly (*Wanna lift?*)

Since I like my morning walk I signalled what I thought was *No* in Colombian taxi-speak: waggling my index finger back and forward a couple of times. The result has been the taxi drivers slamming on the brakes to wait for me.

So now I just shake my head and that seems to be working. Of course I could just ignore them but that seems *so* rude.

CONVERSATION AT THE HAIRDRESSER'S

Young woman: So do you have a boyfriend?

Me: No.

YW: Would you like a Colombian man?

Me: Yes, if he was the right one.

YW: Well, there are good Colombian men, I just don't know them.

Me: Do *you* have a boyfriend?

YW: Yes.

Me: So how is that possible?

YW: Colombian women just have to forgive, over and over again.

Ouch!

UNLIKELY CHAT-UP LINE ON THE BUS TO THE AIRPORT

Man: Excuse me, but are you eating a cardamom sweet?

Me: No.

Man: I thought I could smell cardamom, and it's so long since I've tasted it.

Me: No, sorry.

Man: I thought you might be able to give me a cardamom sweet.

Me: No, sorry. I don't have anything for you.

And that was the end of that conversation.

GOOD NEWS FROM THE AUDIOLOGIST – COLOMBIAN STYLE

I had got this idea that I was losing my hearing, so I went to get my ears tested.

Well, I had nothing to worry about, and the technician and the audiologist, being Colombian, both told me so in a typically flamboyant way:

The technician: "There is nothing wrong with your hearing! Your hearing is perfect. You can hear everything. You can hear my thoughts. You can hear things in the future."

The audiologist: "Your hearing is perfect. You have the hearing of a baby. You have the hearing of a 15-year-old."

BRIEF ENCOUNTER IN THE DEPARTURE LOUNGE AT MONTERÍA AIRPORT

Middle-aged man: Excuse me, do you know if there are toilets here?

Me, engrossed, watching a DVD on my laptop, taking an earpiece out of one ear: I don't actually but I am sure there will be. Try down there.

Man: Thank you. Would you mind keeping an eye on my rucksack?

Me: Sure.

Man leaves and returns and says thank you.

Twenty minutes later, man leaves for his flight and says, "Thank you so much for your company and for being so helpful. Have a good flight."

Anywhere else in the world, I might have thought he was being sarcastic, but no, he was just being Colombian.

INTERCULTURAL COMMUNICATION

Conversation in a shop on the Coast (echoing a conversation my parents had in Peru 45 years ago):

Me, pointing at a bottle of 7 Up: Can I have Siete Oop please?

Old Man, mystified: What?

Me: Siete oop?

Young man, coming to old man's rescue: You mean Seven Up?

Me: Yes. [To old man]: What do you call it?

Old man: Sprite.

CONVERSATION IN THE GYM

Me: How have you been?

Old man: Getting better.

Me: Oh, have you been sick?

Old man: No, I aim to get better every day. You have to face everything with a positive attitude.

WHAT THE PASTOR SAID

On this last trip, I met one of our great friends on the Coast, a pastor who is in charge of scores of churches in an area very much affected by the conflict. "Sister Fiona, I think you are getting fat," he said. "I know," I replied, but then I have been on the Coast for five days," (=eaten lots of rice!).

"No, no, it's good that you are fat," he went on, "it means that people at home will know that you are prospering here in Colombia."

I *am* prospering here in Colombia but I would rather not get fat to prove it.

HOW WOULD YOU HAVE RESPONDED?

1. Context: The hairdresser is telling me about her teenaged son.

"And Thursday is the day the bin [the trash] goes out and when I got home, he hadn't done it, so I took the bin and went to his room and threw it at him."

2. Context: The man fixing my computer is telling me about his little girls.

Me: And do you live with them?

Him: No. I made a mistake and their mother couldn't forgive me.

3. Context: In a taxi. We pass some indigenous people from Ecuador, dressed in their Sunday best, beautiful in their lacy white blouses and long black skirts.

Taxi driver: Look at them! Tidy, hard-working, well-organized. Not like our indigenous people, sitting around on the pavements, begging.

A GOOD MAN IS HARD TO FIND

I'm chatting to a single Colombian woman. We agree it's good not to rush into anything, just for the sake of being married.

"And anyway," I say, "A good man is hard to find."

"Yes," she agreed. "I'd say two out of ten."

UPSIDE DOWN WORLD

One day, I had just printed a stack of materials for our Clubs and a female volunteer and I were carrying the box between us to the nearest metro station. We passed a row of taxis waiting for a fare.

A taxi driver said loudly: "What's the world coming to when the taxis stand empty and women are carrying boxes?"

SHELTERED LIFE

"In fact," I said, to a group of children's club leaders, "the most violence I ever witnessed was in Scotland, not in Colombia, when I saw someone get out of a car and assault a young man waiting at a bus-stop, punching him in the face, and breaking his nose."

"That's the worst thing you've seen?" a leader responded, not unkindly. "I've seen people slashed with machetes, people who've been shot, people who've had their throats cut."

"I know," I said, humbly, "I've led a very sheltered life."

CONVERSATION WITH A BOY

Me: What can I pray for you? What's your dream?

Boy: To go to school.

Me: How old are you?

Boy: Fifteen.

Me: Have you ever been to school?

Boy: No.

HEART-BREAKING CONVERSATION WITH THE HANDY-MAN WHO FIXED MY LITTLE GREEN CASE

He fixed the zips on my little green case, then sat on the floor and mused, "So you're off to your country…Must be nice to travel, see the world. Imagine, I know Copacabana (a municipality outside the city of Medellín) and some parts of Medellín and that's all."

"So you've never been to the beach?" I ask.

"Never. Well, you know, on a minimum salary, it's hard to make ends meet. But I'm not bitter, gold and silver is mine, says the Lord, and I give it to whom I please, I just try to do my job the best I can, serving you all, with a loving heart."

TEN SECONDS OF MY LIFE

I was waiting for the bus one day when two people passed by, pushing a heavy trolley, probably a fast food stall. One was an older, heavyset woman, and the other a young man. They were both putting their backs into the pushing. As they passed, the young man turned his head and stared at me with ferocious intensity. What did it mean? Was it: "How dare you sit at ease, waiting for your bus, while I have to toil here?" I have no idea. And no way of knowing.

FEELING AT HOME

A long time ago I lived in Tain, in the north of Scotland. I remember I used to buy a particular newspaper at a newsagent's, and I knew I had arrived in the town when the lady behind the counter handed me my paper without me having to ask for it. I remembered that today when the lady serving me at the Metro reached for the particular ticket that takes me to my place of work without me having to ask for it.

"Oh, you recognised me!" I exclaimed, "Now I really am at home."

CONVERSATION WITH MY FLATMATE

She said: That outfit makes you look like a missionary.

I said: I know that's not a compliment.

If you are interested, I was wearing a bleach-spotted black T-shirt from a mission I went to in 2008, black and white striped back-packer trousers from Ecuador and flat, black shoes. No make-up and no earrings.

At least everything matched.

CONVERSATION WITH AN HONEST BEGGAR

An old man sits with two small black Labradors at his side, and begs.

He says, "I was hungry where I used to live (a town about 170 kilometres away from Medellín) and I didn't have food for my dogs. Oh, how they looked at me with big, sad eyes. But here, I'm fine. The people are kind and generous. I have my little room, but I don't have anything to do all day, so I come out to the street. Oh, I was hungry before but here there is more than enough food."

117

CONVERSATION IN THE GYM

Sometimes I bump into a genial older gentleman at the gym and this week we got chatting. The conversation went something like this:

Older gentleman: So what is it you're involved with?

Me: A project to train churches on the Coast to look after the children in their communities.

OG: Oh, very good. And you're teaching them values, good things like that?

Me: Yes, that they have value, that their lives have a purpose.

OG: (Without missing a beat) You're naturally blond, aren't you?

Me: No, this is more or less my natural colour.

OG: Oh, you should dye your hair blond. Light eyes and blond hair, you'd look lovely.

Me: I don't think I could cope with the extra attention in the streets.

OG: Oh, you should do it.

Me: Maybe one day.

GOLD

At the weekend I met one of those people whose worth shines through immediately. He was a young lad, probably in his mid-twenties, working in a church plant in a small town on the coast.

Here's a snippet of the conversation with him:

Lad: You see, I'm a *campesino* (a peasant farmer) and it's hard for us to get an education. But my father supported me, thank God, and I was able to complete the course at the Bible Institute.

Me: So were you able to live peacefully on your land all this time?

Lad: Oh, no. In 1995 things got very difficult and we had to leave our farm for two years and just survive on bits and pieces. I was just little but I remember it was very hard. We lost everything, all the food ready to harvest, everything. The house fell into ruins. Then in 1997 my father had the guts to go back and he's worked his land there ever since.

Humble, determined and committed, utterly unsung. How good to know that in the end, the last *will* be first.

RANDOM MOMENT

This week I accompanied a friend to a medical appointment.

After she went in, an older lady sat beside me and started to talk.

"Oh, I'm terribly nervous about this," she said, so first I said, "Oh, you mustn't worry, they're professionals, they know what they're doing," and she said, "I work in the health system and I know they make mistakes," so I then said, "Would you like me to pray for you?" She was thrilled with this. First she prayed, and then she said, "*Arranca, hermosa*" (= Go for it, sweetheart) so it was my turn to pray. All in about five minutes.

TACTFUL (NOT)

I have recently lost some weight (just by eating healthily and taking exercise, nothing drastic) and I have had a lot of fun with people's reactions. In the UK someone who knows me well might say, "Oh, you're looking good. Have you lost some weight?"

Here, acquaintances say things like:

"Oooh, here comes Fiona Lite," (patting my tummy).
"Hello, Barbie."
"Fiona's going to get married now!"

And best of all, someone who met me a few years ago said, not to me directly, but within earshot, "I remember her as being fat."

Not a tactful lot.

RANDOM CONVERSATION

Colombian Number 1: Where is it you're from?

Me: From Scotland.

Colombian Number 1: Can you play the bagpipes?

Me: No. It's hard to play the bagpipes.

Colombian Number 2 to Colombian Number 1: That's like you going to Scotland and them asking you if you play the accordion.

Colombian Number 1: Oh, if they did that, I would say, 'Give me the accordion here,' and I'd give it a go.

CONVERSATION WITH A PASTOR

I have been away the last couple of weekends at camps for our children's club leaders.

Last weekend, I met a remarkable pastor who partly supports himself by growing rice, the staple crop of the area we were visiting.

This is part of the conversation I had with him:

Me: So do you own land?

Pastor: No, I rent the land I farm. I used to have two hectares but I started sending my children to school and one year I didn't have the money to pay the school fees so I sold my land. I decided I was going to get my children an education. I didn't get one. My parents were of the generation who said, 'We didn't get an education and we're still alive,' so I didn't go to school. I started my education when I started walking in the paths of the Lord. I did primary and secondary with my wife, as an adult. But

I made sure my eight children got to study. So that's why I don't have land.

A CONVERSATION IN THE QUEUE FOR A TAXI AT THE SUPERMARKET

The older lady beside me received a phone call on her mobile from someone who was obviously concerned about her.

"I'm fine," she said, "I'm just getting my toenails done. Don't worry, I'm absolutely fine. Thank you for caring but I'm fine."

When she hung up, she turned to me and said, "Oh, why can't people just leave me alone. A whole life of being with people and now I just want some peace and quiet. My son, my daughter-in-law, even my ex-husband all phoning because I'm not at home. On a little innocent outing. Imagine if it was something not so innocent. Forty-eight and half years of marriage and I never went anywhere and now I just want a little freedom. Is it too much to ask?"

"Forty-eight and half years is a long time," I said.

"Yes, but it had died a long time before. I could say it was born dead. We were just two tourists trying to get along. And now I'm 73 and I feel my life has gone by in a flash."

MEETING ON THE METRO

I got chatting to a blind guy on the metro the other day. We talked about different things: his blindness (from an infection a few years ago), how much the metro helps him get around the city, my impressions of Colombia. When we parted he said, "Maybe we will meet again in the darkness."

CONVERSATION WITH A COLLEAGUE (BEFORE THE UK GENERAL ELECTION IN 2017)

Me: Oh, I am so excited about our election on Thursday. It's so hard to predict what's going to happen.

My colleague: Really? Here we usually know beforehand what the result will be.

Me: You see, we are voting for all the MPs, so there are the results of hundreds of constituencies to be announced. The polls close at 10pm and then there is a race to see which constituency declares first, and then they are coming thick and fast, they cut away from one declaration to bring news of another one, it's very exciting.

My colleague: Wow, it sounds like a reality show!

WITNESS

On Saturday I did some Child Protection training in a church in Medellín. When I arrived, I met the mother-in-law of the pastor and she started reminiscing about the time when the neighbourhood was affected by the terrible violence that swept through the city in the 80s and 90s.

"Yes, we have seen lots of things here…For example, there are bullets in the columns of the house…when the builder came to build the walls, he got one out but the others were stuck. Once, someone tried to extort money from us, they said we had to pay them two million pesos or they would kill us. So we started praying and fasting, that was four days, Wednesday, Thursday, Friday, Saturday…and on the Saturday, the man who was extorting us was shot dead. And the dogs who licked up the blood died because the bullets were poisoned."

My Church

THE FIRST YEAR and a bit that I lived in Colombia, I attended and appreciated a small Lutheran church that met in the chapel of the Seminary. After a while, I realized that I was beginning to find Seminary life a bit claustrophobic: I ate and socialized with my students and attended a church 200 yards from my house. In short, I needed to get out. I visited several churches but didn't feel particularly at home in any of them. Over Easter 2009, I visited a friend in another city and attended the Presbyterian Church there. That prompted me to visit the Presbyterian Church in Medellín where I was given a warm welcome by a dear old lady called Doña Estér, and felt instantly at home. The church building was in a very down-at-heel part of Medellín. In fact, it is the only church I have ever attended where the smell of marihuana wafts through the windows.

I discovered that many people in the church had been displaced by violence from the Coast, and that the church was the oldest Protestant church in the city, planted by North American missionaries in 1889 in what was then a prosperous part of town. The aim was to reach the elite of the city with the *gospel. Alas, the neighbourhood sank into destitution before that aim could be fulfilled. A very elderly lady once told me the story of the church. In the early days, people would come from all over the city to attend the church but as Protestant denominations moved into outlying neighbourhoods, the numbers attending fell substantially, until in the 1980s when Presbyterians displaced from the Coast arrived in the city and sought out the familiarity of their denomination.*

I appreciated that I was never expected to do anything, that the church was interested in and supportive of my work with Vive and that I could get an inexpensive lunch there every Sunday.

CONVERSATION IN CHURCH

Older man: Are you from the Coast?

Me: No, I'm from Scotland.

Older man: Married, single, widow?

Me: Single.

Older man gestures to me and back to himself.

Bystander (in a whisper): He's special.

ANOTHER CONVERSATION IN CHURCH

I asked an older lady in church where she was from and this is what she said:

"Well, we were displaced. Sixty-two years ago. At the beginning of the Violence. In those days it was the Conservatives against the Liberals, and we were Liberals and my mother was a Protestant, which made things worse. They killed my father, and burnt our house down. We were meant to have been in the house when it burnt down, but the people who were meant to do it were acquaintances of ours, so they put us in a truck, and said, 'Get out of here, and never come back because if you do, they'll kill us.' We weren't rich, but we had land, we grew coffee, and yucca, and different kinds of banana. It was hard, sometimes we had to sleep on the pavement, and three months after we were displaced my little sister was born. But I must say, the experience made us a strong as a rock and here I am as a witness to what happened. And God never abandoned us."

THREE CONVERSATIONS IN CHURCH

1.
Me: So how are you?

Older lady: Much better thank you. What I think is, if I don't have the illness that is going to kill me, I'll get better.

2.
Me: You're Sebastian, aren't you?

Little boy: No, I'm Santiago! I know your name.

Me: What's my name?

Little boy: Fiona, like the Princess in Shrek.

3.
Me: What have you been up to?

Young man: Picking coffee.

Me: And how is the harvest this year?

Young man: Very poor. They couldn't pay me very much.

CONVERSATION IN CHURCH WITH THE FIRST PERSON WHO WELCOMED ME

Me: So, Doña Estér, how many children do you have?

Doña Estér: Thirteen made it to adulthood but two have died.

Me: So did you have babies who died?

Doña Estér: I lost five babies.

Me (doing the math): So you were pregnant 18 times?

Doña Estér: No, 17. I had twins, too.

I could only say: Doña Estér, I admire you very much.

THE SERMON I HEARD BEFORE I GOT TO CHURCH ON SUNDAY

Place: a taxi
Preacher: the taxi driver

"Have you heard of Martín Emilio "Cochise" Rodríguez? The cyclist? He said, 'More people die in Colombia of envy than of cancer.' He was right! And you know why that is? Because everyone lies. The paramilitaries lie, the guerrillas lie, politicians lie, priests lie. And why do they lie? Because we can't face the truth. We can't face the reality around us.

The guerrillas, negotiating peace in Havana and going on killing! How can they do that? If you want to be with God you have to leave these things, you have to change your life. You know, Colombia is owned by five families. They are against narco-trafficking so they put all their energies to stop it. You know, if drugs were legalized tomorrow, the conflict would end. I'm Catholic you know. I pray every day that God will keep me close to him. You know, sometimes I even have to preach to Christians (=Protestants).

Well, here we are. You're very welcome."

ANOTHER SERMON I HEARD BEFORE I GOT TO CHURCH ON SUNDAY

Yesterday, Palm Sunday, we met a procession of palm-waving pilgrims as we drove down the hill from my flat.

The taxi driver commented, "That's my church but I don't agree with the processions. It's just a re-creation, I don't see the point of it. What's important is to know God's plan of salvation and to listen to the words of Christ... I've been to Mass already, I've been talking to God – that's what the Mass is for us, talking to God – there's just one thing I don't agree with – it's the confession. I think all that is just between God and me... Well, here we are. Have a nice day."

TAXI RIDE TO CHURCH

A street vendor puts a strawberry air freshener on the passenger seat, the taxi driver sniffs it but doesn't buy it. The traffic lights change and the vendor has to sprint down the line, collecting his wares. A car stalls and we squeeze around it. "Take your time, relax, don't worry about the rest of us," the taxi driver says sarcastically to the driver of the stalled car.

Another street vendor offers us chewing gum for 100 pesos. Further along, another taxi and a motorbike have had a little bump, and the taxi driver is gesticulating angrily at the man on the motorbike, who looks a bit abashed, but unhurt. Finally, a drunk or drugged man wanders around in front of us, waving his arms in distress.

Then I arrive at church.

ANOTHER TAXI RIDE TO CHURCH

So today, one of the streets I have to go down on my way to church was closed off, and just as I was working out an alternative route, I spotted two Seminary students who go to my church getting off a bus. I paid the taxi driver, and jumped out of the taxi, yelling their names all the while. We discovered why the street was closed: a bicycle race. The peloton swished by in one direction, and then in the other before we could cross. A man was sleeping on the pavement, sitting up, jacket over his head. I chatted on to cover my embarrassment as we passed the scantily-clad prostitutes, and so we arrived at church without further incident.

A STRUGGLE IN CHURCH

So on Sunday I was sitting in church behind a street person who spent the service lovingly examining and chewing a fingernail on his left hand, I mean really gnawing on it with great gobs of glistening saliva. And all I could think was, "I have to shake that man's hand and I have to do it without showing any repugnance". So I started thinking about Jesus touching the lepers. But when the service ended he shook hands with about ten other people before getting to me so I didn't get the brunt of the gloop.

CONVERSATION IN CHURCH

Colombians are often fascinated by tales of Scotland's cold weather and what it is like to live in a country that has seasons. On Sunday I was explaining to a friend in church what it was like to have very little daylight in winter and almost no darkness in the summer.

"Well, it's very different here," he responded. "Night and day are almost exactly the same. We don't have social equality here but at least we have…" He groped for the right expression.

"Solar equality?" I suggested, and we agreed that was a good way of describing it.

TAXI RIDE TO CHURCH

So last Sunday this is what I saw on my taxi ride to church: A block away, I saw a crowd of people around someone lying on the ground. The glimpse I saw as we passed was of a man on the ground, handcuffed and with blood on his face. A block later, as

I drew up at the church, I saw an old woman, slumped on the pavement, her leg at an odd angle, with a curious crowd around her too.

The worship music booming out of the church rang a little hollow.

CONVERSATION IN CHURCH

Scene: Lunch at church.

Me, looking round the group of youngsters (and always wanting to find connections): This is the table of the only children.

Girl beside me: I've got nine brothers and sisters.

Me: On your father's side?

Girl: Yes.

Me: And do you see ever see them?

Girl: Three of them. One was really old, like forty-five or something, and he died already.

THE RELUCTANT DALMATIAN

The children took the service at church today.

I especially liked the grumpy sunflower, the Dalmatian that had to be shooed into the ark, and the fact that Noah's sons' wives contributed to the building of the ark by bringing their husbands cups of tea.

WORK

Yesterday in church we had to pray for the person beside us, and my partner was a 15-year-old lad.

"What can I pray for you?" I asked.

"That I'll be a good boy and that I'll never leave the paths of God."

So I prayed that for him and then I asked him to pray that God would help me in my work.

This is what he prayed:

"Dear Lord, thank you for Fiona. Please help her in her work. Help to get on with her boss (in Spanish *el patrón*) so that he doesn't say anything against her. Help her not to get sacked and help her to be someone in her life."

Revealing, don't you think?

Urban Ghosts

I ONCE TOOK A PHOTO of someone sleeping on cardboard under a blanket on the pavement opposite my church. Something about the little foot that was sticking out made me think the person was a woman. It made me think about the many people who sleep on the street and their value to God.

Barefoot and homeless,
they sleep like dead men on the streets of the city.
Their past reduced to bundles they use as pillows.
Discarded like the rubbish they rifle through every day.

Everyone should have a home.
Everyone should have shoes.

No one is rubbish.

Storm into a calm

I WROTE THIS IN CHURCH one day when I was going through some turmoil or other.

The rocks, yet Jesus sleeps.
I clutch the gunwale, look with narrowed eyes.
Doesn't He care?
How can He sleep?
I could die here,
Lose all, drown in my fears.

Wake up, Jesus, don't you care if I drown?

He wakes, looks around, reads the situation with one glance.
"Shut up," he says, and at once all is calm*.
"Where is your faith?" he asks. "Why can't you trust me with this?"

It's true, I can't. Or at least, I don't.

Forgive me unbelief.
Forgive my foolish presumption.

That if I think about it a lot,
I'll get further than if I rest in you.

That if I imagine every possible outcome, I'll find peace.

Wake up and say to the fears in my heart, "Peace, be still."

Be the Lord of my heart.
Let me say, "Who is this? Even my pain and confusion obey him."

Show me what to pray.
Show me what to do and give me grace to do it.

Change the storm to calm.

I once had a colleague who was a bit of genius with languages. He was reading the New Testament in Greek and was tickled that a possible translation of Jesus' words to the storm, often translated 'Peace, be still", was "Shut up!"

Gorse

THE WAY A SCENT reminds you that you are far from home.

There are seven shades
of hibiscus on the path,
and one stolid, homely gorse bush.
Picking a flower,
I smell the coconutty smell of home.
It crumbles into petals I can carry,
and press in my diary.
Scotland is not so easy to be had.

Home Leave

HOME LEAVE IS A TRICKY THING FOR MISSIONARIES. *First, we look forward to it immensely, or I certainly did. The opportunity to re-connect with friends and family, being free from the constant vigilance required by life in Colombia, the chance to rest, it's a wonderful thing. My Colombian friends and colleagues thought it was three or four months of holiday and said as much.*

But it often brought stresses and strains of its own. I had to consider with whom to be in touch. Who were the people I definitely had to see and who would make the cut if I had time? A horrible two-tier way of thinking about friendship became inevitable. Then, you had to pack in as many speaking engagements as you could, because each one was an opportunity to pick up supporters. I was always extremely well-supported financially so I didn't feel the pressure as much as others, but to this day, I will take any opportunity to speak in public if it means I can raise a little money for Vive. There was the feeling of the clock ticking from the moment my feet touched Scottish soil, an urgency to make the most of the limited time.

HOME LEAVE 2013

ANSWERING THE QUESTION, WHAT'S IT LIKE BEING HOME?

SEPTEMBER 2103

It's great. Everything is familiar. I can speak the language. I still know my way around, although the 66 bus is now the 6 in Glasgow. It's peaceful and safe. Living with my parents in a quiet Glasgow suburb, I don't hear one single sound at night, and not many more in the day. It's cold but I like the variety of weathers Scotland offers, the way you never quite know how the day is going to turn out.

But it's strange. Everything is the same but I'm different.

WHAT CAN YOU SEE?

SEPTEMBER 2013

Where are you reading this? Outside? Near a window? In a public place? On public transport? In a shopping mall? At an airport? Look around. What can you see? A policeman? A security guard? A soldier? What about weapons? A handgun? A semi-automatic? A taser? A truncheon? Nothing?

This has struck me again, very forcibly. Security in Scotland, in everyday life, is incredibly low-key. No security guards checking your receipt as you leave the supermarket; the army away on foreign wars; the police, unarmed and scarcely to be seen. It's not like this in Colombia.

Oh, that one day it would be!

IT'S SO QUIET!

SEPTEMBER 2013

Have you ever noticed that when you cross the Meadows in Edinburgh, and you are about half way across, you can hardly hear the traffic. In fact, if you listen very carefully, all you can hear is the pad, pad, pad of hundreds of pairs of shoes.

SELF-EVALUATION

NOVEMBER 2013

How should a missionary evaluate the effectiveness of a meeting she speaks at?

Is it by the number of people who attended? Or in stark monetary terms: the donation that follows, the people who sign up to support her financially? Or the number of people who come up to her at the end and say, "That was wonderful"? Or the number of people who dab their eyes at the sad stories? Or the number of people who sign up to get the prayer letter?

Should that question even be asked? Should effectiveness be the aim at all? Is the result of a missionary meeting something hidden, like leaven in flour?

TOP SIX QUESTIONS I GET ASKED

NOVEMBER 2013

I am about half way through my talks round the country and am starting to see a pattern in the questions I get asked.

Here are six questions I have been asked more than once:

1. Is it safe in Colombia?
2. Do you feel safe in Colombia?
3. Is there opposition to your work?
4. Is there persecution of Christians in Colombia?
5. What's the health service like?
6. What's the education system like?

In answering them, I always find myself waffling on a bit in a way I find annoying in other people.

WHAT HAPPENS IN BUCHANAN BUS STATION AFTER DARK

NOVEMBER 2013

A sign on a building in the centre of the bus station concourse reads: *Watering Point for Vehicles.*

I know the reality behind the sign could not be more prosaic but something about the wording conjured up for me the watering holes of the Serengeti Desert: great herds of wildebeest and elephants, and yellow and blue buses drinking their fill as the sun goes down.

I'M ALL MISSIONARY-MEETINGED OUT

DECEMBER 2013

Well, that's me officially finished my talks for the year.

I spoke about my work in Colombia 25 times.

I spoke to about 700 people.

I spoke in two Scottish Episcopal Churches, one Church of Scotland, one Baptist Church, and 14 Free Churches. I spoke at the Latin Link Scottish Conference, the *Freie Evangelische Gemeinde*, Trier, Germany, and to groups in two independent churches.

I spoke at two interdenominational meetings.

Ten of the talks were to women's groups.

I spoke to one Sunday School.

80% of my audience was over 50.

Two thirds of my audience were women; a third, men.

And the moral of the story is: as with the East End, you can take the girl out of the Free Church, but you can't take the Free Church out of the girl.

HOME LEAVE 2016

GLOBAL VILLAGE

FEBRUARY 2016

Recently I got the opportunity to speak to a group of children aged around ten about the life of a displaced child in Colombia. I explained how armed groups force people off their land and talked about the poor conditions displaced people often live in. After my talk, one ten-year-old boy came up to me and asked if the members of the armed group had been radicalized. I explained, "No, they don't have any particular ideology, they are probably motivated by greed as much as anything else."

Afterwards I thought:

1) How good to see a child trying to make sense of the world in terms of the categories (e.g. radicalization) that he knows.

2) How sad that a ten-year-old growing up in a peaceful country has to engage with such things.

But then, when I was ten, I worried about nuclear war.

COLOURS

FEBRUARY 2016

In winter, Scotland's cities and towns can be a bit grey but the countryside is spectacular. The hillsides are covered with coppery brown bracken. The pasture lands are lime green, the lochs slate black. An icing-sugar dusting of snow on the hills. The palest of greeny-blue lichen shavings on the birch trees.

Sometimes, I just had to put on the brakes and say, "Wow".

GREAT QUESTIONS

MARCH 2016

It's always very interesting to hear people's questions in response to the talks I do in churches.

Sometimes I incorporate the answers into later versions of my talk. One example is "How do churches manage to get children to come along to the Vive Kids children's clubs?" I say that in most cases there are scores, if not hundreds of children in the local community and most seem thrilled to come along to an event being run especially for them. The little joke I make is that you just need to shake a tree and 10 children will fall out of it. (Of course we don't really do this!).

But last week I was asked two excellent questions by the same person that left me thinking. Their questions were:

1.What has been the impact of the conflict on the church in Colombia?
2.What are the strengths and weaknesses of the Colombian church?

I thought these were very useful questions for any context. For example we could ask: What has been the impact of the recession (or the refugee crisis) on the Scottish church? What are the strengths and weakness of your local church? Or your denomination?

I don't feel I had very coherent answers to the questions but the questions themselves were great!

My Ode to Autumn

THIS IS MY ATTEMPT to write a 'proper' poem, whatever that is.

O people of the further north,
I wonder if you know the worth
of autumn? The gold, shorn fields,
the bramble hedge, the harvest moon,
the final burst of summer flowers,
and trees of green and red and brown.
Go out, take breaths,
deep breaths of cool, sweet air,
and think of those, far off,
where days plod on, each one the same,
whose only change is hot to wet.
Be glad you live with seasons.

Eavesdropping

I DON'T DELIBERATELY LISTEN IN to others' conversations but sometimes people speak so loudly and what they have to say is so entertaining that I can't help myself.

INTRIGUING OR WHAT?

Slightly raggedy man to more raggedy man, walking quickly past where I was standing at the bus stop:

"In your case, if they say you're mad, there'll be a psychological assessment…"

OVERHEARD IN MEDELLÍN

In a café, one older woman to another: "You'll need to take lots of warm clothes; Switzerland is colder than France."

In a café, a father trying to regain the custody of his child to two legal advisers: "I don't think one traumatic event damages a child, does it?"

On the metro, a young man to his friends: "And then he kills these women and makes perfume from them."

(Don't worry, it's the plot of a book, *Perfume*, by Patrick Süskind).

OVERHEARD AT THE AIRPORT

"You know, stuff at airports is notorious for being overpriced. They have a captivated audience."

AT BOGOTÁ AIRPORT

A father was telling his young son the story of the Spanish Civil War. I think it was a family story, maybe the child's great grandfather had escaped to South America when Franco took power. The father was using the tone of voice reserved for myths and legends, and the child was fully engaged in the story, asking questions every so often.

At one point he said, "It's good that Hitler died, isn't it, daddy?"

IN NEW YORK

Boy: Let me explain what happened. I didn't want to crash into that man.

Older dad: I understand. But you were still scootering too fast.

One woman to another: And then Eric woke up one morning and decided he didn't want to be married any more.

Mum to son, reading the caption on the exhibit: Whales evolved from land animals.

Son, in a voice of utter disbelief: Whales evolved from land animals? Whaaaaaaat?

AT A CLASSICAL CONCERT IN SCOTLAND

"So she put her feet up on the seat, and she was like seventeen, so…whatever….and this guy came up to her and said, 'This isn't Glastonbury.'"

ON THE TRAIN IN SCOTLAND

"So I'm going to Mexico in 362 days."

"362 days?"

"Yes, I've got an app that tells you how many days it is till your holiday. Anyway, my mum said, 'Mexico, isn't that dangerous?' And she asked me which area I was going to because a man had been attacked in Mexico on a golf course somewhere. So I said, 'Don't worry, I won't play golf.'

OVERHEARD ON THE TRAIN IN GLASGOW

Context: a conversation about Christmas presents for the kids.

"One thing I find is that the stockings get smaller as the kids get older, I mean the presents sometimes cost more, but it looks less, so you feel guilty."

AT THE BUREAU DE CHANGE IN GLASGOW

An older Glasgow lady is getting a currency which has some exotic script on it, maybe Arabic.

She gets a little plastic bag for it which she tucks in her handbag.

"I'll put that in for him with his copy of *Viz*, she says [a rude, adult magazine]. It's a good thing they don't know what it is, or they'd chop his head off."

ON THE TRAIN IN SCOTLAND, A MALE SPEAKER

"It's funny how your mind works: I don't remember the whole night out, I just remember the fish supper."

ON A BUS IN EDINBURGH

Two men in front of me, strangers to each other and the city, bonded over the weather and their shared experience of being parents.

One was recovering from a painful illness and this is what he said:

"Well, you pray when you're in pain, don't you? I'm Church of England, but I believe there's something out there, a supreme being, there has to be. It's like when you are on a plane and you start to pray 'Lord, just get me down from here, and I'll be a good boy,' and then you land and you forget all about it. It's dreadful, really."

AT PANAMA AIRPORT

Colombian woman to a Mexican woman:

"No, we're in a mess, I can tell you. Things are very bad. The violence, the corruption. Only God can help us now. Things were bad and then Uribe came and made us feel safe, but now…"

OVERHEARD ON THE METRO IN MEDELLÍN

A young woman is talking on her mobile phone. She is talking in a quiet, almost monotonous voice. This is what she is saying:

"They took the motorbike, some papers. They got in through the balcony, they were using the place to sell drugs, and I don't like that. They are actually my neighbours. They took the television and the sound system, and all my university papers, and I went to the police to report it, and then they threatened me so I had to leave. If you'd like I can come to you and we can talk about it face to face."

And then it was my stop and that was the end of the story for me.

OVERHEARD IN ECUADOR

1. BRITISH SPEAKERS

"They built a road near us and everybody got compensation to put double-glazing in their houses, and we looked at each other and said, 'Holiday,' and that's when we did the Grand Canyon."

"We did two months of bed and breakfast in Canada and we didn't have the same breakfast twice."

2. US SPEAKERS

"When I started my job four years ago, on the very first day, someone was shot outside the school."

OVERHEARD AT THE SWIMMING POOL IN SCOTLAND

From their voices, they were eight or nine years old, but I didn't see them.

Speaker A: I'm not wearing my school socks, look. I hate my school socks.

Speaker B: So do I! They're so annoying.

A: I'm putting all my clothes in my bag.

B: I'm not. My bag is SO small.

A: So you and Tanya are like related?

B: Yeah.

A: Because you are the same religion?

B: Yeah.

A: I don't really know about religion because I don't have one…People who have a religion have to respect people who don't have one.

B: And people who don't have one, have to respect those who do.

A: Yeah. It's the same for everyone.

OUTSIDE MY BEDROOM WINDOW IN MEDELLÍN

Outside my bedroom window, I heard a woman explaining, as if to a child: "You see, the thing is that most babies are cute."

THE DELIVERY MAN

One day, my flatmate ordered a home grocery delivery. When I opened the door to the delivery man, I discovered that he was talking, seemingly to himself. But he was not crazy, just talking on a hands-free phone. Which he continued to do as he brought the bags in.

And this is what he was saying:

"Listen, sweetheart. He's fine for just now. Enjoy yourself. That's fine. But you and I both know that he is not the man for your life, not the man to make plans with. He can be your boyfriend for now, that's OK, but you know that long term this isn't going anywhere."

TWO SCHOOLBOYS ON THE TRAIN TO EAST KILBRIDE

One says to the other, "And they put peas in leek and potato soup."

Obviously not the done thing in the leafy suburbs of Stamperland.

OUT AND ABOUT IN THE UK

Man on the phone: "I've eaten salmon twice today but I'll happily eat it tomorrow."

Man on the phone to the mother of his son: "You need to go over his six, seven, eight and nine times tables."

Inaudible voice must say something like: "Where will I find them?"

Man: "From your head preferably…"

Female student to male travelling companion: "It's that she won't because she can't because of her religion."

A LITTLE INTERACTION IN A CORNER SHOP IN GLASGOW

Two teenagers were breathlessly telling the lad behind the counter, who was obviously a mate, about something that had happened. From what I overheard I think they must have built or made something, I imagine a hide or tree house or some such thing, and someone – a woman – destroyed it. They even had photos on their mobile phone to prove it.

Then the guy behind the counter asked, "Was she old?"

And one of the teenagers said, "Forty."

But I couldn't tell from their tone of voice if that meant yes or no.

Blogs about Spanish

ALL LANGUAGES HAVE THEIR DELIGHTS but I found Colombian Spanish wonderfully rich and varied.

HOW DO YOU SAY IT?

Do you have a saying for when someone stands between you and the TV? In Scotland we say, "You'd make a better door than a window." In Bogota they say, "Your dad didn't make windows." On the Coast they say, "Donkey meat isn't transparent."

COURTEOUS COLOMBIANISM

If you say thank you to a Colombian waiter, he might respond, *"Para servirle."* It literally means, "To serve you," (as in, "I'm here to serve you,") and I think it sounds so CUTE.

HOMONYM

I think it's funny that in Spanish *muñeca* means both doll and wrist.

DOUBLE SCULLS? FENCING?

I speak pretty good Spanish, (I should, I grew up in Peru, and I studied it at university) but every so often I find my communicative competence challenged, and just now it is the Olympics that are doing it.

Federer broke in the first game of the set but Falla broke back.
Britain won a gold medal in the double sculls rowing.
Venezuela is on for a gold in the fencing.
They usually start showing the split times once everybody has started.

…are all ideas I have struggled to express in Spanish over the past few days. But at least I've learned that set point is *set point* in Spanish.

YOU CAN'T TEACH AN OLD DOG NEW TRICKS IN SPANISH IS...

...an old parrot doesn't learn to speak.

QUIRKY

A friend was telling me about a situation she had faced in the past and she said, "There wasn't enough hair for a ponytail." From the context I think it means something like "I felt out of my depth, I didn't have the skills for the task."

IT'S A SMALL WORLD **IN SPANISH IS...**

...the world's a handkerchief.

TO THROW THE BABY OUT WITH THE BATH WATER **IN SPANISH IS...**

...to throw the baby out with the nappy.

BROCHA Y PINCEL

This week I was editing some materials for our children's clubs, and suddenly I was six years old again.

My colleague had written the words *brocha y pincel* as part of the resources required for the lesson. The words both mean paintbrush, but one is thicker than the other. Anyway, when I was a six-year-old primary pupil in Peru, our teacher told us we had to bring *brocha y pincel* to class the next day. I dutifully passed the message on to my mum, and I set off to school with a paintbrush and a press-stud. "What a funny combination," we thought.

To this day, I remember my teacher holding a paintbrush and the press-stud out to me and explaining, *Esto es una brocha* (paintbrush) *y esto es un broche* (press-stud).

And so began a lifetime of never quite understanding what was going on.

NEOLOGISM

The Spanish I hear around me is remarkably free of English influence. People just do not tend to drop English words into conversation. But I have noticed that one English word has found a foothold in Colombian Spanish and it's the word *play*. It has nothing to do with its meaning in English. In fact, it has even changed its part of speech and is now an adjective meaning *great*, *cool*, *fantastic*.

For emphasis you can even say that something is *súper play*.

HOW EASILY DO YOU FALL ASLEEP?

There is no end to the vivid, delightful ways in which people express themselves here.

"I would fall asleep looking after a tiger," a friend says, to describe how easily she falls asleep.

WHAT MEDELLÍN DID

Buenos Aires, Glasgow and Medellín were in the running to host the 2018 Summer Youth Olympics. Medellín was confident it would be successful in its bid but in the end it lost out to Buenos Aires.

It counted its chickens before they were hatched, or as they say here: It mounted the horse before saddling it.

I LOVE LANGUAGE!

The Spanish for the sea is *el mar*.

The Spanish for tide is *marea*.
The Spanish for nausea is *mareo*.

THREE'S A CROWD

You know in English we say someone is "playing gooseberry" when they are the third person hanging out with a couple?

(In German they call it being "the fifth wheel on the car").

In Colombia they say you're there, "as the violinist".

WHAT THE GUIDE SAID

I had just walked six hours to see one of the world's highest waterfalls, the spectacular Gocta Falls, in the north of Peru, and we were within sight of the village where we were going to have lunch, when I stood on a wobbly stone and fell over in a most undignified way.

The local guide helped me up and said, "The bread burned in the door of the oven," meaning things went wrong almost at the end of the journey.

Little harm done, thankfully.

ONLY GLASWEGIANS WILL GET THIS

An informal way of saying good bye here is *chao* (pronounced like the Italian *ciao*). If you say good bye to more than one person you can say *chaos*.

TO CALL A SPADE A SPADE IN SPANISH IS...

...al pan pan y al vino vino.

To the bread, bread and to the wine, wine. A bit more poetic than ours, somehow, don't you think?

THIS IS CUTE

My friend was telling me how she learned English: "I didn't go to classes, I just learned the chewing gum way."

She means, informally, just whatever happened to stick.

NEED A WAY OF BEING DISMISSIVE? HERE'S ONE

A friend is talking about a mutual friend's ex-boyfriends.

"Let's face it," he says, "they weren't much use. They weren't even any good for making a stock."

A PHRASE I LEARNED RECENTLY

Here's a picturesque way to say in Spanish that someone has gone crazy: "One of his roof tiles slipped."

HOW VIVID IS THIS METAPHOR?

Almost every day I am charmed by the vividness of the Spanish language. Recently, a friend was talking about friendship – in English we might say, "They are as thick as thieves" – and she said in Spanish, "They are fingernail and dirt."

AS EXPRESSIVE AN EXPRESSION AS YOU COULD WISH FOR

We were out for our team Christmas dinner last night, to a restaurant that serves a special kind of meat from the Llanos region of Colombia.

We all ate loads, but one piece of meat was unclaimed at the end so I asked one of my colleagues if he wanted it.

"Oh no," he said, "I'm so full that even a grain of rice standing up wouldn't fit."

A THROWAWAY, REVEALING COMMENT

There is a word in Spanish – *monte* – which has all sorts of connotations. It can simply mean "hill" but it usually has the additional meaning of somewhere remote. I once saw some graffiti which said something about going to the *monte* and I could tell from the context it meant "going to join the guerrilla".

It can also mean "vegetation" – as in the case of El Salado, the town I visited back in 2011 which was abandoned after a massacre. When the people returned, they found the town full of *monte*.

At the youth event last week, a group of youngsters were acting a drama, and the star, a lad of about 15 called Luis, got frustrated at the lacklustre performance of his peers and said,

"I'm the one from the *monte* and I'm acting much better than you who are all from the town."

161

IN MY ELEMENT

You know how in English we say, "I was in my element," to mean, "I felt really at home, I felt comfortable,"? Well, today I found out how to say this in Spanish. My colleague was telling us about a trip he had made at the weekend to a gold-mining town in the north of Colombia. The trip involved hours on bad roads and river-crossings in boats, basically all the things we love.

"I was in my sauce," he said.

The Street

THERE WAS ALWAYS SO MUCH street life to see, sometimes from the bus and sometimes at eye-level.

GLIMPSES FROM THE BUS 1

There is a lady who begs at a set of traffic lights on my bus route to work. She is elderly, and leans on a Zimmer frame, and begs from the drivers of the passing cars. One day I saw that someone had given her a 1000 peso note (worth about 35 pence sterling or 55 US cents), and she crossed herself with it.

GLIMPSES FROM THE BUS 2

Two boys on bicycles, aged about 12, have hooked themselves on to the back of a truck, and whizz along a busy road. Their faces have a look of extreme concentration, and they need to be on their toes, because if the driver of the truck brakes sharply, they're dead.

GLIMPSES FROM THE BUS 3

A goose-stepping Chihuahua. Honestly, that's exactly what it looked like.

GLIMPSES FROM THE BUS 4

Yesterday from the bus I saw a young policeman gently kick the ankle of a man sleeping under a bridge in the centre of town (a kind of wake-up call for the poor). The man wearily raised his head. He had survived the night and was alive to struggle on another day.

GLIMPSES FROM THE BUS 5

Someone is sleeping on the street with a motorcycle helmet on. I guess it stops it being stolen, and prevents him having his head stepped on, but wow, it must be hot inside.

FEET

A homeless man made himself a little shelter from cardboard boxes under the flyover down the hill from my flat. All I could ever see of him were his bare feet, and I could only tell that he wasn't dead, because his feet were in a different position every day.

BUS RIDE TO WORK

One day this week I paid attention and this is what I saw from the bus on my way to work:

an old man crouched over rubbish, recycling. He's just found a torch, which he checks to see if it works, then stores in a plastic bag.

a poster asking for help to find a missing poodle called *Luna* (=Moon).

a mum getting her little boy ready for school with that universal maternal gesture of a lick to the thumb and a wipe of the face.

angry graffiti: *Education for all or for none! Don't vote! Fight the system!*

I SEE FROM THE BUS

…two boys aged about 10 and 12 juggling with machetes.

A Colombian peasant farmer lives with his machete strapped to his thigh. With it, he can clear a field, peel a mango, and whittle a point as sharp as a needle. Now his sons, perhaps reduced to penury by displacement, use the family's machetes to entertain the people who wait at Medellín's traffic lights.

THE NEVER-ENDING RESOURCEFULNESS OF THE STREET PERFORMER

There is a new trend in street performance: the high-wire act. A rope is strung between two posts alongside the traffic lights, and the artist juggles while standing, precariously, on one leg on the rope. Yesterday, through the bus window, I could only see the performer's legs, one adjusting all the time to the tension in the rope, the other held out to maintain his balance. His juggling clubs started appearing, about waist-high, changing colour as he rotated them; the traffic lights changed and when he jumped down from the rope, I saw that he also had a football, but I have no idea what he was doing with that, maybe balancing it on his head. He dashed along the line of cars collecting coins; just another participant in Medellín's endlessly varied and beautiful street life.

PROACTIVE STREET VENDING

There is a group of young men who ply their wares at traffic lights. They wait until the lights turn red, then work their way down the queue of cars, placing their merchandise (maybe pirated DVDs or packs of pens) on the dashboard of the first six to eight cars. When the lights are about to turn green, they dash up the line, collecting the product, or the money.

Their stress levels must be spectacularly high.

HOW TO MAKE A LIVING ON THE STREET

You can beg, simply asking for money, but my impression is that this is only tolerated on the street if you are very old, or disabled. You can beg, adding a true or invented story, usually involving illness.

You can hit the tyres of cars with a stick to see if they need air.

You can wash windscreens.

You can help cars get parked outside restaurants, by waving a red cloth to direct them into the space.

You can fill potholes with earth and charge drivers to pass.

You can hold the door of a taxi open or carry a suitcase across the road.

You can entertain, by singing, rapping, juggling machetes or fire, telling stories or riding a unicycle.

You can sell: chewing gum, sweets, lighters, peanuts, sunglasses, cell-phone chargers, educational books, cigarettes, pirated DVDs or, most lucratively of all, yourself.

WAYS OF MAKING A LIVING ON THE STREET

Here are a couple of vehicle-related ways of making a living on the street:

THE TAXI HUSTLER

If you arrive at an empty taxi rank, these lads will run out to the nearest main road, and hail a taxi for you. They then run into the rank with a proprietorial hand on the taxi, hold the door open for you and often call you *Madre* (=Mother). It is expected that both you and the taxi driver will give them a coin.

THE BARRIER REMOVER

A roundabout at the bottom of my hill is closed off with movable barriers during the week. For a fee, some lads will move the barrier for you, so you don't have to make the annoying detour two blocks down.

This is Colombia

I WAS ALWAYS on the look out for moments that illustrated some deeper truth about Colombia, both for myself and for the readers of my blog.

AT THE AIRPORT

Medellín airport is, like most things to do with transport here, clean and efficient. The arrival and departure boards work. All you need to do to get to where you need to be is to follow the directions. However, on my recent trip to Cali I noticed that just about everybody coming through departures checked their gate number with a member of staff.

My deduction? Here, the personal relationship is everything and official information is inherently untrustworthy.

MY FIRST COLOMBIAN WEDDING

I thoroughly enjoyed my first Colombian wedding.

The only man wearing a tie was the photographer. The bride was beautiful and wore orchids in her hair. The notary who carried out the civil ceremony encouraged the couple to have children, but to plan their arrival carefully, so that they could afford to educate them to be productive Colombian citizens.

CHAOS

In other times of my life and in other places, I have lived fairly tranquilly, and I have seen turbulence as something to be endured to arrive at a renewed period of tranquillity. But in Colombia there is no tranquillity. No day is like any other. It may be because something great happens, or something terrible, or just something unusual. But there is no normal, no such thing as an ordinary day.

There is no enduring of turbulence to achieve tranquillity.

There is only embracing of the chaos.

WHATEVER NEXT?

A couple of weeks ago, resourceful thieves in Barranquilla, Colombia's fourth-largest city, used slices of watermelon to slide an ATM out of the chemist's they were stealing it from.

DISPUTE

A dispute between Colombian air traffic controllers and the government has led to airlines cancelling and delaying flights in protest.

It's called Operation Tortoise.

PHILANTHROPY

My shopping comes to 19990 pesos (about 7 pounds sterling or 11 US dollars). I pay with a 20000 peso note. "Would you like to donate the 10 pesos to our foundation?" the cashier asks. "Oh, go on then," I say. One third of a British penny, half a US cent.

If I had said no, she would have had to give me 50 pesos in change, because that is smallest available coin.

How does any business ever balance its books?

YOUNG MAN, OLD MAN

Two men take turns to cut the grass outside our office, one old, one young.

The young one, so young he is scarcely out of school, is up and coming, willing to work hard, and won't be cutting grass all his life. The old one, walks with a limp, pulls his mower on a little cart, and is followed everywhere by an old dog.

I see him passing and think, "Life is such a struggle for some people."

My colleague sees him passing and says, "Oh, I hope he doesn't ring our bell to ask for work, because it breaks my heart to say no."

COLOMBIA'S GOT TALENT

On tonight's show, there was a man whose talent was to eat a sandwich while riding a bike. There was a lad doing astonishing things with a spinning top. There was a group of jugglers, who formed a pyramid while they juggled. And there was a man whose entire act consisted in stopping his heart for a few seconds.

REVEALING REACTION

It's funny watching Downton Abbey in Colombia. For a start, I don't know how to translate words like footman, kitchen maid, valet, or Dowager Duchess for the local audience. And the Colombian tendency to be prepared for the worst means that watching the series can be a tense experience. Example: John Bates and Tom Barrow meet unexpectedly in the dark. "He's going to kill him," gasps my fellow-viewer.

In reality, they have a philosophical little chat and no one is harmed.

CASUAL RACISM

I am buying something in a shop and the till is slow to respond. "Oh, it's just being a bit Indian," the shop assistant says cheerfully.

Note: That's a casual slur against Colombia's indigenous people not the citizens of the nation of India.

GRAFFITI

Someone has painted Exodus 20 (where the giving of the 10 commandments is recorded) in green paint on an underpass. Presumably because *Thou Shalt Not Graffiti* isn't one of the commandments.

HOW I KNOW I HAVE ADAPTED TO CULTURE HERE

I go into a little shop near our office to buy milk. The lady is clearly still serving the man ahead of me in the queue, but I ASK FOR WHAT I WANT ANYWAY. Shop assistants here serve multiple customers but until now I haven't felt comfortable jumping in with my request before the person ahead of me had completely finished their purchase. But now I do. It's just taken three years of living here.

PAGANINI PAISA STYLE

During Medellín's annual International Music Festival I went to a free concert of Paganini's 24 Caprices for solo violin. I liked the announcement that was made before the concert began: "If you need to be in touch with someone by mobile phone during the performance, you are not in the right state of mind to be at a concert."

And in fact the audience listened in rapt, appreciative and respectful silence, with not a mobile phone to be heard, apart from two moments: the first, when a string broke on the soloist's violin and the second, when she played a particularly showy section. When the string broke, the audience cheered and clapped until she returned. It seemed that this moment had many elements that Colombians appreciate: drama, serenity in the face of adversity, and an indomitable spirit.

In the showy section, we all said, "Ah!"

REVEALING REACTION

We are watching a sweet Italian film about a little boy who loses his sight in an accident and is sent to a special school. In one scene he is shown playing around on a bike along with a sighted friend. They run into a demonstration (this is Italy in the 1970s) and talk to some of the students.

"Oh no," says the person with whom I am watching the film, "they are going to steal his bicycle!"

I'M ALL PARADOXED OUT

There is a nifty system in place in Medellín's interchange metro station, San Antonio. Those arriving on one line leave by one set of door and stairs, and those joining the train wait on the other side on metal bridges. (The only exception is when it is raining. Then those joining the train are allowed to wait on the other side so they don't get wet.) The other day I was walking down the stairs to join the other line, when a policeman raced up the stairs to catch a man coming up the wrong side. With an embarrassed grin the wrongdoer immediately turned back.

In other words: Zero tolerance = very effective.

But it got me thinking about impunity in Colombia, thoughts that went something like this:

Man goes down wrong stair in the metro: instantly caught. Hundreds of thousands of women abused in the conflict: very few convictions, and 82% of victims don't even report the crime to the authorities.

SWEET TOOTH

A man rummaging in the rubbish for anything of value asks me for a coin. I shake my head and in that moment he finds a catering-sized tub of *arequipe*, Colombia's delicious sticky, sweet, caramel sauce. He pops off the lid and gets to work with a grimy finger, extracting what has been left behind and enjoying it with lip-smacking relish.

TO-DO-LIST

Some time ago, I found this forlorn little to-do-list in my notebook:

Get new cédula [my Colombian ID card].
(1st week in Feb.)
1st week in March.
Sometime, never.

Here's why: when I got my visa last May, I immediately applied for the ID card. I got a paper version fairly quickly, with the promise that I would get the plastic one in January. The paper one was stolen in November with my other documents [I was pickpocketed in the Medellín metro], but the Immigration

Office told me not to worry as I could just collect the plastic one in January as planned.

When I went to the Office in January, they told me the system had changed and I needed to come back in February. When I phoned in February, they said my card wasn't ready and to contact them again in a couple of weeks. By March, I got so discouraged, I stopped phoning. In May, I summoned all my energy-for-facing-bureaucracy and went to the office again. They took my photo and my fingerprints, all ten, electronically, and told me my card would be ready in two weeks.

Yesterday, on 19th August, I picked it up.

A JOKE

I need a new car.
What makes you think you need a new car?
I stuck my hand out of the window to indicate and someone put a coin in it.

DON'T TAKE ILL AT RUSH HOUR

Last week I was on a bus stuck in a traffic jam, and a taxi came up behind us, horn blaring, forcing the two lanes of traffic apart to get past. All the motorbikes around it started beeping, too. As the taxi passed, I could see someone writhing in the back seat. In lieu of an ambulance, the taxi driver was doing his heroic best to get the patient to the hospital on time.

CULTURA METRO

The Metro in Medellín is clean, safe and orderly, and a mammoth effort goes in to keeping that way. Yesterday I was amused to see a metro official approach a young man and hand him a leaflet containing the seven rules for using the Metro.

His crime?

He had stepped on the yellow line designed to keep passenger back from the trains.

Long live the cultura metro!

WOMEN ARE HIGHLY REGARDED IN THE METRO SYSTEM

Announcement on the metro

(This is not my translation – it is announced in English by a sweetly-accented Latina woman)

Women are highly regarded in the metro system. Treat them with courtesy and respect. Never overstep the limits of propriety.

At least that's what she wants to say, but the last word comes out as "property."

ON THE METRO

Two interesting people sat opposite me on the metro last week.

One was an immaculately dressed businessman, reading a book called *Generating Wealth*.

The other was the only person I have ever seen in Colombia wearing a hijab.

The seat between them stayed empty.

IN CASE OF ACCIDENT

I see a lot of accidents as I travel about Medellín, maybe two or three a week, and mostly involving motorbikes. The protocol in Colombia is that the vehicles involved can't be moved until the traffic police have arrived to take the pictures and measure the braking distances and so on. Of course, the result is a massive jam.

But one detail I have observed that I really like is that the drivers of the cars (if they are unhurt) get out and greet each other with a handshake before they start any exchange of insurance details or business like that. You may have just been involved in an accident but you are jolly well going to observe Colombia's courteous culture!

CONTRAST SEEMS A BIT OF A WEAK WORD TO DESCRIBE THIS

Yesterday evening I went to a wonderful concert featuring a choir of about 40 young people. They sang beautifully in eight languages and all without the words or music. The languages were Greek, Latin, German, French, Portuguese, Spanish, Embera (an indigenous Colombian language) and an indigenous Bolivian language. The standard was very high, in my humble opinion. The concert hall was right in the centre of Medellín. The minute we stepped outside the venue, we were back in Colombia's other reality, the rough sleepers already cocooned in their makeshift shelters, the night workers just starting their working day, busily searching through the rubbish, selling, begging.

Everywhere in the world you can find these contrasts if you look hard enough, but in Colombia, they are side by side, all the time, and the effect can be just a little mind-blowing.

HOW I KNOW I AM IN COLOMBIA

Yesterday morning, it took me half an hour to choose my clothes. In Scotland, I checked the weather, decided how many layers I needed to put on and rummaged for clothes, almost at random. Here it has to be an outfit!

It's called cross-cultural adaptation.

BACK IN MEDELLÍN

I got back to Medellín [from Scotland] on Tuesday evening. Everything went like clockwork on the trip, if you don't count my dad's car getting a flat tyre on the way to the airport.

Yesterday evening I got a taxi to meet my flatmate as she finished work so we could go out for a belated birthday meal. It was rush hour. The driver was one of the very aggressive, lane-changing, foot-on-the brake jamming, horn-tooting breed. I lived on my nerves the whole way. People stepped out in front of us. Motorbikes wove in and out of the lanes of traffic. Buses pulled by, perilously close. It's amazing what five months in sedate wee

Scotland can do to one's perceptions. "I get used to this, every time," I had to remind myself, as I got out of the taxi, knees trembling.

I didn't quite kiss the ground.

I CAN'T BELIEVE I SAW THIS

On my way to work, I walk down a steep hill. It's one of the main roads into Medellín from the south, called *Las Palmas*. Today, I saw a man on a motorbike tootling down the hill, singing at the top of his voice. AND CLAPPING HIS HANDS. With gusto. Not for a millisecond either, for at least several seconds, until he swung round the corner out of my sight.

EVERYONE'S A DRAMATIST

Last week I took a taxi and I only had a 50,000 peso note (worth about £12) with me. The correct etiquette is to tell the driver that when you get in so if he doesn't have change, he can solve the problem before the end of the ride. So in this case, the driver drove into a petrol station and asked one of the men working there if he could change the note.

First, the man made the dramatic Colombian cut-throat gesture which means "I'm broke." But he wasn't, he just wanted to make a wee drama out of the transaction. He took my note and held it up to the light. "No, this is fake," he said. But it wasn't, he just wanted to milk the situation for a second or two longer.

Then with a smile, he gave the driver the change and we went our separate ways.

CHEERFUL, CREATIVE RESOURCEFULNESS

Here are two stories about Colombians' amazing capacity to take on a task and in no time and with very few resources, produce something beautiful and worthwhile. Today's story is about something that happened on our mission retreat at the beginning of October. September is the month of love and friendship in Colombia, a bit like Valentine's Day for the whole month but including friendship as well as romance. Work colleagues, church youth groups and families play "Secret Friend", a bit like "Secret Santa" in which you buy a present for someone in the group and when you open your present you have to guess who it is from.

Anyway, we decided to play Secret Friend at our retreat but without spending any money. I took a box of scrap paper and ribbons and Sellotape and pens, and everybody had to make something for someone else in about an hour. The results were spectacular: a Bible verse stitched into a leaf, origami flowers, a booklet, cards with thoughtful messages, envelopes decorated with flowers... No one complained that the task was silly and everyone was thrilled with their gift, even me, who received a stone, apparently because "I am both fragile and strong."

More of evidence of Colombians' general awesomeness comes from the camps we hold for our leaders every year. The camps run from Friday evening to Sunday lunchtime and the Saturday evening is the time for the leaders' talents to shine. Last year, we studied the life of Paul and the leaders were divided into groups to dramatize episodes from his life, which they did with great gusto. This year we upped the ante, giving the leaders the task of developing one area of our new Child Protection Policy and then presenting it in some dramatic way.

The areas were things like:

- who should be a children's club leader and what process should they undergo to be accepted into the team.
- what should be our policy with regard to photos and other information about children.
- how can we ensure that every leader has the necessary training in this area.
- how can we ensure that children are safe at all times in a Funky Frog Club.
- what steps should we take in the case of misconduct and what the repercussions should be.

Quite tricky things! But the dramatizations were brilliant, often getting to the heart of the problem and as a bonus, showing me what the leaders had already internalized in the previous Child Protection Training. There was some wonderful improvised acting, clever scenarios even some multimedia presentations.

All done cheerfully, in very little time and with virtually no resources.

BANCO DE LA REPÚBLICA

Here is a funny "only in Colombia" moment that happened a few weeks ago. Some time ago I inherited a bag-full of small Colombian coins, 10 and 20 pesos pieces, which are no longer in circulation, a couple of old 50 peso pieces (worth about 1p) and an old coin that I couldn't identify. In the interests of wrapping up neatly everything in Colombia, I set off on a quest to find out if I could get these old coins exchanged. First, I asked in the bank in which most of my friends have their accounts and they told me that coins could only be exchanged in the *Banco de la República*. I asked there and was told that I could come between 8am and 10.30am. When I returned at the appointed hour, the guard looked dubiously at my little bag of coins and told me to go upstairs.

There I joined a queue of people with huge sacks of coins to exchange for notes. When it was my turn, the clerk counted out my little pile of 20 peso pieces without blinking an eye and noted what they came to. He exchanged my old 50 pesos. He identified the old coin as "*centavos*", in such a shocked voice that I understood he couldn't do anything with it.

And then, he counted out my 10-peso pieces and discovered that there were only 9. He rummaged in a drawer, retrieved one 10-peso piece from his stash, added it to my pile, and added 100 pesos to my gains.

It all came to about a thousand pesos and my reward for all that perseverance was a rarely seen, new, thousand-peso note. "Next time," the man said, "please separate out the older and newer 20 peso pieces." Alas, there will probably not be a next time, but thank you, anonymous clerk in the Banco de la República, for attending to my ludicrous request so graciously and allowing me to wrap up that piece of unfinished business.

It's raining

BECAUSE SOMETIMES a moment is so perfect you just have to write it down.

It's raining.
Raindrops fall at random.

The leaves ping up
like struck cymbals,
played by tiny
invisible hands.

Travel advice for Colombia you won't get in a guidebook

CROSSING THE STREET

In case you ever have to cross a street in Medellín, here is some advice:

1. Get in some training. You will have to run.
2. Get in a group. There is safety in numbers.
3. Watch for motorbikes. They sneak up between the two lanes of cars. Peak round the corner of the first car before committing yourself.
4. Pray. I'm not kidding.
5. Make eye contact with the driver of the car you are dodging past. He will be much less likely to knock you over if you have established some sort of relationship with him.

CULTURAL NORMS

If you want to show how tall a person is, especially a small person, you indicate it with your hand sideways, not with the palm facing down. Showing height with your palm facing down indicates the size of an animal, and it's quite rude to use it when talking about a child.

HOW TO GREET A COLOMBIAN

If you are a woman, it's relatively easy to know what to do: kiss the right cheek of the person you are greeting, that is, lean to the left. Just one kiss. To be really authentic, don't kiss the cheek, kiss the air beside it. If you are a man, you kiss the women, and shake hands with the men. But if you know the man well, you can hug him without embarrassment, slapping his back for good measure.

Confusion only arises as a foreigner when you meet another foreigner. *Do we do what Colombians do or revert to national type?*

COLOMBIAN FAREWELLS

Colombian farewells work much the same way as Colombian greetings: hugs and kisses all round. But I have observed something: the good-bye kiss on the cheek HAS TO BE THE LAST THING THAT HAPPENS IN THE INTERACTION. So, you are winding up your conversation. It's time to say goodbye, so you do. But wait, you've just thought of something else to say. You say it. And now the rule is, you have to kiss again, even if only seconds have passed since the last time.

It's as if the interaction has to be safely trapped between the beginning and ending kisses.

AVOID THE EXHAUST

When you get on a *mototaxi* (that's the motorbike taxi service which is the most common – and hair-raising – way to get around in the towns on the Coast) make sure you get on the side away from the exhaust.

HOT

If someone says somewhere is *caliente* (=hot) they are not necessarily talking about the weather.

[*They mean it's dangerous, which I didn't bother adding on my blog, assuming my readers could work it out for themselves*].

ON THE BUS

When you get off a bus, check behind you to make sure a motorbike isn't sneaking round the inside.

WHY POINT WHEN YOU CAN POUT?

And why say 'pardon?' when you can wrinkle your nose?

Colombians have two cute habits, one I have learned the other I haven't quite mastered. Rather than pointing with their fingers (considered quite rude, I think), they point with their lips and a particular tilt of their heads. I do this too, now. And if you say something they don't quite catch, they wrinkle their noses. But I'd feel silly doing that.

GETTING OFF THE BUS

If you ever need to get off a bus in Medellín, here is some helpful advice.
1. Plan ahead. You might have to push pass about 20 people to get to the door.
2. Have your money in your hand to pay the driver as you get off. You don't want to be rummaging in your bag for your purse.
3. Apologize quietly to everybody whose toes you stand on. They will all say, "Don't worry about it."
4. If the bell doesn't work, say, "Here, please, sir."
5. If someone is sitting on the step, tap them gently on the head to get their attention.
6. Don't be offended if a complete stranger gives you his hand as you step off.
7. Thank the driver.

TAXI SEMIOTICS

A flash of lights or a toot of the horn can mean, *Are you looking for a lift?* or, *You're pretty*, or, *You ran out in front of me and gave me a fright.*

The hazard lights mean, *I've seen you, and I'm stopping.*

Conversations with taxi drivers

I TOOK HUNDREDS OF TAXIS in Colombia and very often the drivers were remarkable people, with a story to tell, an opinion or prejudice to express, or an insight about Colombia to offer.

PREJUDICE

A car cuts in dangerously in front of us. The taxi driver hoots his horn, and the driver of the car in front belatedly indicates.

"Now he indicates," I say.

"Let me tell you something, the driver of that car is definitely a woman. Not that I am *machista* but a man would never do that," the taxi driver replies.

"Let's see if we can pass them and check," I say, but unfortunately, the car has tinted windows, and I don't have the chance to confound this chauvinist with evidence.

CONVERSATION IN A TAXI

The conversation begins with the taxi driver telling me that he had a heart attack three months ago. He tells me about the ins and outs of his care, his battles with his health insurers, the disagreements his doctors have had about his care before finally telling me that his cardiac rehabilitation will start the next day.

CLASSICAL MUSIC

I was in a taxi last week and the music on the radio was classical, one of Mozart's horn concertos, to be precise. This is very unusual here where Latin rhythms predominate. I say how much I enjoyed the music and the driver replies, "Yes, classical music relaxes me. And if I get bored with classical music, which I never do, I play country."

TIME FOR A REVOLUTION

I am bumping along Bogotá's terrible roads in a taxi when we hit a particularly deep pothole.

"How can you stand this?" I gasp.

"We're screwed," the taxi driver replied. "We are living under a monarchy."

"A monarchy?" I ask, intrigued.

"Corruption," he replied.

ON THE RADIO IN THE TAXI

"You know, I am really disappointed, really fed up with the world. Remember I was asking for people to donate blood for my friend? Well, people actually phoned him up and said they would sell him their blood for $100,000 (=£34, $55). Isn't that terrible?

But we are Christians and we are going to bless these people. Lord, we pray for your blessings to be showered on these people, material blessings, health, bless them, Lord.

Let them always have enough blood in their veins…"

IN A TAXI

Last night I'm in a taxi talking on my mobile phone: "So you've got a landline, well, why don't you give me the number and I'll phone you when I get home, let me just note it down…" Just as I begin to rummage in my handbag for a pen, the taxi driver hands me a piece of paper and pen.

Am I:
a) annoyed that he is listening to my conversation
or
b) impressed at his helpfulness?

Mainly b, I think.

GET ME TO THE CHURCH ON TIME

Last weekend I was invited to a wedding and, although my head told me there was no way it would start at 4pm, as stated on the invitation, my punctual Scottish soul (yes, I still have one) just couldn't count on it. So I set off in a taxi in plenty of time to get there at 4pm. About seven minutes out, we hit a huge traffic jam. We waited for about ten minutes to see if it would resolve. In that time I phoned two friends who were also invited. Both were still in their respective homes, just starting to think about leaving. Eventually the taxi driver worked out that he could get me there by another route. "Have you done this trip before? How much do you usually pay?" he asked.

"12 to13 thousand pesos," I said.

The new route worked and I got there at about 4.20. The meter had gone over 15,000 but he would only take 13,000. "No, no, that was the deal," he insisted. "It wasn't your fault we hit that jam, and it was mine even less," he said.

There were about 15 people there when I arrived, and the wedding, which was beautiful, got started after 5pm.

LEAVING TOWN

"Oh no," the taxi driver said. "The roads round the bus station are all blocked and the roads out of Medellín in every direction are closed."

I was accompanying my colleague to get her bus back to Sincelejo on Colombia's Atlantic Coast when the taxi driver gave us the bad news.

"Well, the bus company said it was OK," I said.

"Oh, well," the taxi driver said. "Just commit yourself to God and you'll be fine."

We made it to the bus station no problem at all. As we waited, buses started arriving, turned back by demonstrators supporting the farmers' strike, who had blocked the road north.

"We heard shots," someone was reported to have said.

"The road might be opened in an hour or two," the bus company said. And it was. My colleague finally got away at about 10.30

Moral of the story: don't believe everything you hear.

CONVERSATION WITH A TAXI DRIVER IN LIMA

Him: So where is it you're from?
Me: From Scotland.
Him: Oh, yes. Where's that exactly?
Me: In Europe. To the north of England.

The taxi driver goes quiet for a bit, and taps away on his smartphone. I imagine he is checking the traffic ahead or some such taxi-driverly necessity.

Then... Him: Ah yes, I see, all together on one island.

He's been looking up Scotland on Google Maps.

ANOTHER EAVESDROPPING TAXI DRIVER

In the taxi on the way home from the cinema, my flat mate was telling me that she had mislaid a book and couldn't think to whom she had lent it.

"We had that problem when I was growing up," the taxi driver chipped in. "We were always lending things, things from the kitchen, tools, things like that, and not getting them back, and eventually we got a notebook and attached a pencil to it and noted down what we lent and when we got it back we scored it out. And then one day someone borrowed the notebook and didn't note it down and we lost it."

A ONE-SIDED CONVERSATION IN A TAXI

A routine taxi-ride to the cinema (to see *How to Train your Dragon 2*).

The taxi driver starts telling me something and I can't understand a word he is saying. But that doesn't stop me nodding and saying "uhuh" and generally keeping my end of the conversation up. Half way through I had a guilty thought that I should ask him to repeat himself, paying him the courtesy of really trying to understand what he was saying.

But I didn't.

THE PATRON SAINT OF TAXI DRIVERS

Yesterday (16th July) was the feast day of "Our Lady of Mount Carmel", the patron saint of drivers. To celebrate, many taxis, buses and trucks got all decked out in colourful ribbons, forming great, tooting processions at different points around the city.

"How is it organized?" I asked a taxi driver, as we crawled along behind a column of school buses.

"Oh, they have their procession just when they feel like it," he replied. "For example, this lot are taking advantage of the fact that they don't have to pick school kids up until the afternoon."

A COMPULSIVE NEED TO COMMUNICATE

I've noticed I have a tendency to commentate on my taxi journeys. "Very busy time of day," I say.

Or: "This might take a while," as we crawl along. Or: "I think there must be an accident ahead because it's not usually like this at this time." [When we pass the accident] "Ah, I was right."

Why the need to state the obvious? I don't think it has anything to do with what's going on outside, I just have a compulsive need to communicate.

ANOTHER CONVERSATION WITH A TAXI DRIVER

TD: You're foreign, aren't you? North American?

Me: No, I'm Scottish.

TD: And how long have you been in Medellín?

Me: Almost 5 years.

TD: Husband?

Me: No.

TD: Well, I'll tell you what the problem is. It's that us men just don't want to commit. We're afraid, you see, there are so many women out there, so many, that we are afraid of being unfaithful. So my advice to you is to have affairs and not to fall in love.

Me: No, no. I'm waiting for a man who is prepared to commit and if he doesn't come along, I'll stay single.

TD: Why?

Me: Because I want to please God.

TD: Well, that's wonderful. What a sweet thing. Well, I hope that man comes along for you.

RANDOM THINGS A TAXI DRIVER SAID TO ME YESTERDAY

"English?" he asked.

"No, Scottish," I replied.

"I saw a film once about William Wallace," he continued. "He had armies and built up a great empire in Europe. I've driven taxis in lots of different cities. I get the passengers to tell me the routes and that's how I get to know the place. How many people do you think there are in Medellín? Seven million. There's only four million in Panama. Is England in Chicago? Well, it's been a pleasure to have you in my taxi."

CONVERSATION WITH A TAXI DRIVER

Me: So how is it going?

Taxi Driver: Wonderful. You know, I have a very rich Father and he is very generous to me.

Me: Oh, yes?

Taxi Driver: Yes, it's God. He's so good to me. Look, today I've already made the $80,000 I need to make to pay the owner of the taxi. And I always make a good $50,000 on top and I pay all my bills. I've just taken my wife shopping. Oh, I am very blessed. I am Catholic but I am very respectful of Evangelicals – the real ones, not the 11-month ones – the ones who are good all year and then have a big blowout in December.

STREAM OF CONSCIOUSNESS

Another taxi driver made my evening today. He bought some chewing gum from a young woman who was carrying her sleeping toddler over her shoulder and that prompted him to say:

"I really admire these women. See these women, making a living on the street, selling their chewing gum, not prostituting themselves. She doesn't have to pay child care, she's got her child there, where he grows up, he can help her sell. If it were marihuana, that would be different. But chewing gum… Because it's hard you know. I have a friend who sells minutes [for mobile phones] in the centre. And she's not pretty. And men come up to her and say "How much do you make in an hour?" and she says "$15,000″ (=£4 approx.)" and he says, "Look, I'll pay you that, and I'll buy you a nice lunch and then we'll go to a hotel, and I'll give you $30,000," and she's good, she knows how to handle the situation, and she's starving but she says, 'No thank you, I bring my lunch box.' No, there are some women the street doesn't devour, and that's admirable."

A TAXI DRIVER TALKS

"My children are almost grownup. I have one who is nearly a professional. My wife left me three years ago and left me with the children. But I stuck with them. My father didn't abandon me and I didn't abandon them. There is a lady in our block of flats who likes me. I've got a flat, I'm in debt up to here but I pay my way. Anyway, this lady got my son on to the course to be a traffic cop. You know, when you're poor you have to use all the levers you can get. This lady, she's a lawyer with the mayor's office, something to do with traffic and she said, 'I'll get your son onto the course to be a traffic cop.' And my son said he wanted to study Animation in 3D and I said, 'Forget it, that's a course for rich kids, you do this course to be a traffic cop, and start earning 2 million pesos a month (about £550). Then if you want to study, you save up and you can study later on.'"

JOURNEY HOME

It's getting harder and harder to get home any time after about 5pm.

Yesterday, the taxi driver asked me where I was going and reluctantly let me get in and only then realized that he had confused my hill with another less congested one but by that time I was in the taxi and I wasn't going anywhere.

"Look at that," he grumbled, as we passed the gridlocked traffic on the way down the hill.

"How about you let me off at the filling station and you can keep going up rather than getting stuck coming down?" I (most magnanimously) offered. "I don't live very far up the hill, it's quite easy for me to walk."

"OK, then," he agreed.

But then I realized he *was* turning up my hill.

"So you *are* taking me home," I said.

"Oh, the princess has to get home," he said.

CONVERSATION WITH A TAXI DRIVER

One day I was going to church in a taxi and I commented on the "ciclovía", the lane of the main road that is closed to cars every Sunday so that people can run and cycle along it.

From that beginning we got on to talking about sports and which sports we liked doing and which sports we liked watching and then we got talking about swimming pools and whether they were clean.

And then, the taxi driver told me this story:

"A few years ago I worked in a *finca* (a house in the country) and when I got there the swimming pool was disgusting. I cleaned it [insert detailed description of the cleaning products and processes here]. And I got it lovely, with crystal clear water and people came from all around to swim in that pool. In the evenings, when there was no one there, my wife and my children swam in the pool.

One day, the owner of the house (the *patrón*) came to me and said, 'I've heard that your family are using my pool. I don't want you to do that. It's my pool.'

That night, I said to my wife, 'Take the children and go to Medellín and find somewhere for us to live.'

So she went, and thank God, she found a flat right away. That was a Thursday and that weekend I left the country house and came to Medellín and got a job driving a taxi almost immediately and I've been doing that ever since. I worked hard on that pool and to tell me my family couldn't use it, well, I couldn't put up with that."

ANOTHER CONVERSATION IN A TAXI

So a week or two back I had the usual conversation in a taxi.

Taxi driver: You're not from around here.

Me: No, I'm from Scotland.

TD: So you like it here?

Me: Yes, I'm very happy.

TD: Married?

Me: No.

TD: So no one has your heart?

Me: [thinking: I'm a missionary, I'd better make something of this opportunity] Well, God has my heart, I guess.

And the taxi driver took his hands off the wheel and gave me a round of applause!

WELL-TAUGHT TAXI DRIVER

Taxi Driver: What's today's date?

Me: The 22nd.

TD: The world is going to end tomorrow [repeating a rumour that was going the rounds].

Me: Oh yes, that's right.

Five minutes later:

Me: I don't think the world is going to end tomorrow.

TD: Of course not. Only the Father knows the time. Not even the Son knows.

ANOTHER STREAM OF CONSCIOUSNESS

This was more of a stream of consciousness than a conversation and I wish I could do it justice but this will give you a flavour of it:

"I've been driving since five in the morning [it was now 6pm]. I'm tired, I'd like to stop soon. But even then, I have to get the taxi cleaned, get the car to my *patrón*. [His mobile rings]. Oh, [handing me the phone] could you send him a whatsapp to say I'm driving and could he phone me again, thanks. Medellín is getting impossible to drive in. Ten, fifteen years ago, Medellín was wonderful but now, everyone is coming here, even people from abroad, from Germany, from Vietnam, the streets are full, and the drivers are so rude, they don't know how to drive, it's so stressful, for the last five years it's been getting worse and worse but what can I do, I only did up to grade 3 in primary school, I never studied, so I have to drive a taxi and these youngsters they drive for a couple of hours and they complain, I drive all day, I have my lunch and then keep on driving, but they complain, I don't complain. My daughter, she's involved with an Australian, my ex-wife, I'm separated, says, 'Oh, she can't go so far away,' but I say, 'No, let her lead her own life,' and the Australian came, and I can't speak English and he can't speak Spanish but we communicated. The internet's great, you can keep in touch, I have a great big TV, and I go places, using the internet, I do tours of Brussels or Venice, I can travel the world…this is your place? Take a note of my number in case you ever want to call a taxi, lovely to meet you."

The End

The Road to Emmaus

WHEN I WENT BACK TO COLOMBIA *in 2011 my commitment was total. I imagined that I might spend the rest of my working life there and I couldn't picture any future that didn't include that beautiful country. When people asked me how long I was going to stay, I would tell them, "Until my parents need me." As an only child, I felt quite strongly that I needed to be with my parents when they got more vulnerable, something family-loving Colombians completely understood, but that still felt like a long time in the future.*

However, when I was on home leave in 2016, I had a sense from God that I would serve for two more years, and immediately a different future came into focus. I pictured myself returning to Scotland in 2018 in time for the 80th birthday of one of my aunts in April and for my parents' Golden Wedding in July. Then, I thought, I would visit friends in Australia for a once in a lifetime holiday before the next chapter of my life began. Amazingly, all that happened. But in the meantime, I had to face up to my fears of an unknown future:

JOURNAL – MAY 2016

Christ is risen. All is accomplished. All is restored.

But the disciples on the road to Emmaus don't know this. Their knowledge is limited, they are telling themselves the wrong story. What has to happen? How can they get past their sorrow? Because surely they must have cried that day?

They can get past their sorrow by Jesus telling them the story, by him giving them the bigger picture in which the small fragments of their life can fit in. It is only Jesus that makes sense of their suffering. It is only Jesus that makes sense of the facts, the limited facts at their disposal.

The result – a burning heart, transformation, the energy to go back to Jerusalem to share the good news.

So how about your story?

The story I told about myself was: I will get married and have children. That will be the main purpose of my life.

And when that didn't happen, I mourned.

Then I said, "I'll be a missionary to Colombia and work on the Vive curriculum for the rest of my life". That will be my life's work. And when it didn't happen, I mourned.

I am on the road to Emmaus. Everything has been done for me. The happy ending is assured. But I am still in the dark. I need Jesus to explain it all. I need Jesus to break bread in front of me, for my eyes to be opened.

Burnout

THE TWO YEARS *that passed between me understanding that I was to leave Colombia and my departure were very difficult. I was burnt out, suffering from vicarious trauma from listening to so many horrific stories, shaken by some of the political developments locally and feeling far from God. At least, these are some of the labels I can put on what I was feeling as I look back on that time. When I was living through them, my frequent question was, "What is wrong with me?" My writing increasingly reflected that feeling, although occasionally, there was a flicker of hope.*

I wrote this in a church service in Bogotá in November 2016:

The earth was still hot beneath my feet.
The trees were charred stumps.
But the plants were gone,
their frail sap no match for the power of the fire.

I walked on ash,
on charred coals.
Too stunned to cry.

My hands began to work.
I swept, I raked.
Workmen came and felled the charcoal trees.

From one an artist made a sculpture
which is still admired.

One day, when I had long lost hope,
I found a spike of grace, life from the dead.

This time I cried.

Munich

IN DECEMBER 2016 I visited friends in Germany. This is what the transition from Colombia to Europe felt like at that moment. It was actually a lovely time with kind friends and life-loving children and I got some time to myself, which was a gift, too.

I have stepped off the roller coaster.

At least for today,
At least for now.

Not quite at rest,
but at least,
not clinging on, white-knuckled,
eyes clamped shut,
mouth a silent scream.

Today at least
I will look out over the terrain.
I will look up at the sky.
I will breathe more freely.

I have nothing to say.
Your problems leave me cold.
I have nothing to say.

I can begin a phrase...
"In Colombia..."
"Once I..."
"Last year..."

But then I have nothing to add.
I have nothing to say.
Don't make me speak.

I can breathe

I THINK I WAS PHYSICALLY UNWELL when I wrote this in my journal in May 2017, which contributed to my sense of being at an end of myself.

I can breathe
That I can do.
And shower, and make my food.

And open my mouth to say things
I may or may not believe.

But make a plan,
decide a course of action
care about anything.
save myself,
that is beyond me.

Grace

The director of my mission told me about a writing competition where you had to rework a Bible passage. I chose the parable in Matthew 20:1-15. I didn't win but I'm pleased with the story which I published on my blog after I returned from Colombia.

Doña Elena was rich and she liked everything in her house just so. One day, she decided to hire some people to clean her whole house. She went to the market in the morning and spoke to some of the vendors who had bought their produce to sell. "Come and work for me today," Doña Elena said to the first three, "And I'll pay you what you would have made selling your tomatoes, plus a day's pay for a cleaner." The women immediately agreed. They left their produce and followed Doña Elena back to her house. Word quickly got around that Doña Elena was cleaning her house.

The first three women had been working for an hour, washing every piece of glass in the huge chandelier that hung in the *sala* of the house, when there was a timid knock at the door. Doña Elena opened the door and there stood two teenage girls.

"We heard you were cleaning, Doña Elena," one said. "Could we work for you today?"

"Yes, ladies," Doña Elena said. "There is plenty of work to be done. Come in."

She got them started polishing the silver cutlery that Doña Elena's ancestor had brought over from Spain. An hour later, there was another knock at the door. This time, it was an older woman, with a defiant look on her face. "I'd like to work for you today, Doña Elena," she said.

"Certainly, come in," said Doña Elena, and she gave the woman a duster to clean the massive paintings of fruit that hung on the walls round the hallway.

And so it went on all day.

The sun was beginning to set when there was the tiniest knock on the door. If Doña Elena hadn't been passing, she probably wouldn't have heard it. When she opened the door, she saw a child, a girl of about ten.

"May I work?" she asked.

Doña Elena looked about her. What was there left to do? She led the child into the kitchen. In the sink was one china cup.

"You may wash that cup," she said.

The child was too small to reach the tap easily, so Doña Elena brought her a chair to stand on. The child washed the cup with infinite care but even so, the task was soon completed. The other women were beginning to gather in the hall, anticipating their payment. Doña Elena took out a bag of coins. She began with the first three women.

"Here is the money for your produce, five pesos, and ten for the day's work. Thank you."

She then turned to the teenagers and paid them the same, fifteen pesos. She worked her way around the room, paying each one exactly the same amount. Finally, she came to the little girl. There was a tense silence in the room. She counted out fifteen pesos to her, too. One of the first women burst out, "But *patrona*, how can that be fair? We worked all day, from early morning and you are paying the same to all the others?"

Doña Elena looked at the woman and said, "Did I pay you what I promised you?"

"Yes, but…"

"I paid you exactly what I promised. As for the rest, I can do what I like with my own money. Take your payment and go."

One by one the women left. Some were embarrassed and couldn't look Elena in the eye. Others murmured their thanks.

But the little girl flung her arms around Doña Elena's neck and kissed her cheek.

The End and the Beginning

AND THEN, THE FINAL GOODBYES HAD BEEN SAID and there was nothing left to do but get on the plane.

JOURNAL – MARCH 2018

HEATHROW TERMINAL 5

The first day of the rest of my life.

A perfect, pure moment, for the first time in more than 12 years, I don't have a concrete plan to go back to Colombia. I feel as light as a feather.

That weightless feeling – having left miraculously well – and before the reality of the rest of my life kicks in. Before the UK begins to annoy me and before I break any of the resolutions I haven't yet made.

Hoping to hold onto the paradigm shift: we missionaries need to get over ourselves – if I were a Venezuelan refugee, I would have to get work tomorrow or I would go hungry.

…

Resting in the loving arms of Jesus.

Coda

I WAS SO RELAXED as I waited in Heathrow Terminal 5 for my flight to Glasgow that I missed it, inexplicably and expensively, as I had to pay for a whole new single flight. I got a kind and helpful British Airways person to help me, who finished the conversation by saying, "I think everything happens for a reason and someone is looking out for you." Which of course, I agreed with. I puzzled over the meaning of my strange lapse until it was time to get my later flight north. At the gate I met a family friend and that was nice, but I did wonder if it could really be the reason I had paid over £300 for a ticket. I ended up sitting beside a woman who was nervous about flying and we had a lovely conversation all the way to Glasgow. She asked about what I had been doing in Colombia and in the most natural way, I was able to tell her about Jesus.

So began my new life.

About the author

Fiona Lyn Christie was born in Peru to Scottish missionary parents. She studied languages and trained as a teacher before working in the north of Scotland, Moldova and Germany. She trained Egyptian teachers of English in Edinburgh before moving to Colombia to teach English in the Bible Seminary of Colombia in Medellín in 2008. From 2011 to 2018 she worked for the Vive Foundation, training children's club leaders and leading the production of a Bible curriculum for children in disadvantaged rural communities in the north of Colombia.

She returned to Edinburgh in 2019 and now works for a charity that supports people with learning disabilities.

By the same author

RAINBOW WEATHER

A white man dressed as a Xhosa initiate is found dead in the South African countryside. In Scotland, a casual lie is told to impress a new colleague. In Colombia, a friend sows a seed of doubt about a husband's fidelity. The consequences of these three events ripple throughout the lives of three women on three continents and none of them will be the same again.

THE FIRST COLOMBIAN IN SPACE

Viviana Pacheco is five years old when she sees footage of the first moon landing on television. A year later, the circus comes to town and Viviana's life will never be the same again. Set in on Colombia's Atlantic Coast, The First Colombian in Space imagines the life of a child who attends a Funky Frog children's club.

All the proceeds from the sale of this short story will go towards the work of the Vive Foundation and the Funky Frog Clubs.

Printed in Great Britain
by Amazon